DEFINING VIOLENCE

Sang Bradby has endured war and assault. He and his brothers Lawrence and Donald Bradby, have had the kindness and love to support their sister through the aftermath of a sexual assault.

This book is dedicated to all three of them.

Defining Violence

Understanding the causes and effects of violence

Edited by
HANNAH BRADBY

Avebury

Aldershot • Brookfield USA • Hong Kong • Singapore • Sydney

Published by
Avebury
Ashgate Publishing Limited
Gower House
Croft Road
Aldershot
Hants GU11 3HR
England

Ashgate Publishing Company
Old Post Road
Brookfield
Vermont 05036
USA

British Library Cataloguing in Publication Data

Bradby, Hannah
    Defining violence: understanding the causes and effects of
    violence
    1. Violence   2. Women – Crimes against   3. Violence – Research
    I. Title
    303.6

    ISBN 1 85972 108 7

Library of Congress Catalog Card Number: 96-83234

Printed and bound by Athenaeum Press, Ltd.,
Gateshead, Tyne & Wear.

Contents

Figures and tables

Acknowledgements

Chapter 2 by Janette Forman and Jan Macleod, chapter 5 by Billie Weiss and chapter 6 by Anthony Zwi have been developed from papers that were given at the Second International Safe Communities Conference in September 1992. Chapter 4 by Marina Barnard is reprinted with the permission of Blackwells, on behalf of the editorial board of the journal the *Sociology of Health and Illness*, where it first appeared in 1993.

Kate Hunt, Simon Carter and Hannah Bradby are supported by the Medical Research Council. Work on this volume was not conducted in the course of employment by the Medical Research Council and the views expressed are not necessarily those of the Council.

I am indebted to Stuart William Robertson and to Lindsay Macaulay who worked on the manuscript for publication. Grateful thanks go to colleagues, friends and family who have maintained an interest and enthusiasm for this book during its long inception. The authors contributing to this volume and colleagues at the MRC Medical Sociology Unit in Glasgow have been particularly helpful in this respect. Thanks also to David Bradby and Carol Emslie who offered valuable comments on the introduction.

Notes on contributors

Hannah Bradby is a researcher in medical sociology at Glasgow University, and was the Press Officer for the Second International Safe Communities Conference at Strathclyde University in September 1992.

David Stone was born in Glasgow and after qualifying in Medicine at Edinburgh University in 1972, he worked in England and Israel before returning to Glasgow. He has published on public health issues such as screening, health care planning and injury prevention.

Kate Hunt is a researcher working at the MRC Medical Sociology Unit in Glasgow. Her principal research interests are in social inequalities in health (and particularly gender inequalities), and the social construction of gender.

Jenny Kitzinger is a lesbian feminist working at the Glasgow University Media Group. Her current research is on the media coverage of child sexual abuse.

Janette Forman has worked with abused women and children as a social worker with Strathclyde Regional Council. She joined the Women's Support Project in 1990 as a development worker and has completed research on the links between child sexual abuse and domestic violence.

Jan Macleod has been involved in feminist work against male violence since 1978, when she joined Strathclyde Rape Crisis Centre. She was involved in the setting up of the Women's Support Project, and since 1986 she has been a full time development worker with the Project.

The **Women's Support Project** is based in the East End of Glasgow working against violence against women. Its aim is to raise awareness about women's experience of violence such as domestic violence, child sexual abuse, rape and sexual assault and to try to ensure that abused women receive an improved and consistent service. Areas of work include information and advice, training and development, the raising of community awareness through teaching self-defence and offering resources such as books and videos in a lending library.

Marina A. Barnard has moved to the Department of Social Policy at the University of Glasgow, having completed her ethnographic study of Glasgow's streetworking prostitutes while at the Public Health Research Unit at the same University.

Billie Weiss is an epidemiologist by training and works on the Injury and Violence Prevention Program in the Department of Health Services, Los Angeles County. Her latest conference presentations at American and British conferences have concerned gang homicides and assaults in Los Angeles.

Anthony B. Zwi is a public health physician based in the Health Economics and Financing Programme, Health Policy Unit at the London School of Hygiene and Tropical Medicine. He trained initially in medicine in South Africa, and was actively involved in the progressive health movement. He has written extensively around the public health effects of political violence and conflict and is presently researching the health policy options faced by countries after relative peace is secured. He is also actively involved with research concerning injuries, both intentional and unintentional, in developing countries.

Simon Carter is a social researcher at Glasgow University. He completed a PhD at the Centre for Science Studies and Science Policy, University of Lancaster.

Introduction

Hannah Bradby

What is meant by the term violence? Each chapter in this volume considers a particular form of violence in a particular context in an attempt to answer this question. This introduction seeks to consider definitions of violence in the context of the discourses that have constructed particular forms of violence as legitimate. Recent thought and research casts doubt upon these constructions and implies the need for a broader definition.

Violence is a common feature of many people's lives. It has been argued that the ubiquity of representations and actualities of violence and the self-evident nature of many forms of violence constitute a major obstacle to understanding and hence remedying it (Agudelo, 1992). Feminist research on, and campaigns against, violence against women demonstrate the necessity of defining the problem in order to expose it to investigation: only once the battery of a woman at the hands of her partner is defined as illegitimate does prevention become possible.

The definition of a problem determines the solutions that are considered. For instance, when violence against women is constructed as due to men's responses to provocation by women, solutions present themselves in terms of women altering their behaviour. It is argued here that the definitions of violence that are current in social science and public health literature have two features which constrain understanding of the causes of violence. Firstly, definitions of violence are based on an understanding of violence as the use of force by one person against another, or against oneself. Secondly, this force is defined as being employed intentionally (Rosenberg et al., 1992; Kornblit, 1994). It is the interpersonal nature of the model of violence that makes intention so central. Both lay and professional understandings of violence depend upon there being an aggressor and a victim. Thus wars are understood as large scale versions of interpersonal conflicts, with one party viewed as an aggressor whose intention is to harm the other party. The prospect that a war might be due to economic interests is not one that fits into this model.

1

As a consequence of the interpersonal nature of definitions those causes of violence that are not concerned with animosity between individuals or groups of individuals tend not to be considered in analyses. For instance, 'accidental' violence that is viewed as a regrettable by-product of economic systems that has to be tolerated as a 'necessary evil' is excluded. Such instances are important and present a considerable challenge to orthodox analyses of violence in human society (see chapter 7), and are discussed in more detail later.

The central role of intention in defining violence in various contexts makes it worthy of further discussion. This centrality is marked both in legal definitions of violence which seek to attribute responsibility for violence defined as criminal, and in medicine which defines appropriate long term help for victims of violence according to the intentionality behind resulting injuries. As the profession involved in regulating treatment of injuries resulting from violence, medicine has played an important role in constructing our understandings of violence.

In diagnosing and treating an injury the medical profession makes a division between intentional and unintentional injuries. Medicine's interest in the consequences of violence has largely been confined to the physical damage done to bodies and therefore the necessity of the role of intent might be questioned.

The significance of the classificatory division between intentional and unintentional injuries is not only of academic interest as it has implications that go beyond the Accident and Emergency Department of the hospital. The long term treatment offered to victims of violence may vary according to the intention that is diagnosed as lying behind injuries. Intentionally inflicted injuries (for instance, those resulting from child abuse or self-mutilation) have a member of the 'caring professions' such as a social worker or a psychologist assigned to their case. Once the physical wounds are healed counselling or psychotherapy might be offered to treat the accompanying spiritual or psychological damage. By contrast such psychological care is more rarely offered to those with accidentally or unintentionally inflicted injuries such as those resulting from road traffic accidents or house fires, although post-traumatic stress disorder is increasingly recognized (see chapter 1).

The division made between intentional and unintentional injuries is also marked in who is deemed responsible for the search for long term solutions. In general intentionally inflicted injuries are regarded as an individual problem, and hence the solutions envisaged are of an individual order. The problem of intentional injury is dealt with by treating the perpetrator who is assumed to be 'sick' or deviant in some way. Thus self-mutilators must be counselled or psychologically treated and rapists locked up.

In the case of unintentional injuries such as motor vehicle accidents and house fires, the root of the problem is assumed to lie with the physical environment rather than the individual. Therefore road planners and architects are held responsible for curbing the incidence of unintentional injuries.

Feminist campaigns against violence against women have contributed to the central role that interpersonal intention plays in understanding violence. This has been for sound political reasons that stem from the way that violence against women has been constructed as the fault of the woman and not the perpetrator. Therefore a central tenet of some feminist campaigns has been to emphasize the deliberate and premeditated ways in which men carry out violence against women. In terms of the way that cases of sexual assault are treated in courts of law this has been a particularly important move. It has contributed to undermining the myth that men are unable to resist their impulses to abuse women, and that the 'provocative' appearance or behaviour of a woman is more pertinent than the crime of the perpetrator. However, in terms of understanding the longterm causes of violence, especially the way that certain social groups (such as women, children, ethnic minorities) tend to be abused by other social groups (men, adults, ethnic majorities) the emphasis on the intention of the individual may be less than expedient.

The recent Zero Tolerance campaign (see chapter 3) represents a move to make violence against women and children a social problem, rather than an individual one. The 'Zero Tolerance' refers to a society that views all male violence as a crime and does not admit circumstances that have been constructed as extenuating, such as 'provocative' behaviour from women or drunkenness on behalf of men. Thus the emphasis moves away from women needing to 'manage' their men, and on to the law to condemn violence against women. Conversely recent anti-drunken driving campaigns have sought to make individuals feel more personally responsible for the potential victims of drunken driving. Emotive images of both perpetrators and victims of drunken driving imply that the resultant mortality and morbidity is not just an acceptable 'risk' of living in a society with cars, but rather the result of the antisocial behaviour of individuals. This is perhaps the beginning of a blurring of the distinction between injuries for which the purposeful behaviour of individuals is held responsible, and those which are considered to be 'accidental'. However, it is maintained that despite these recent indications of change the classificatory division between intentional and unintentional injuries is a persistent feature of our understanding of violence and that it obscures as much as it illuminates.

3

The 'habit of thinking in dichotomies' such as intentional/unintentional has been described as one of the shortcomings of western philosophy (Sherwin, 1989). This style of thinking that insists on either/or classifications puts an embargo on what has been referred to as 'both/sometimes-the-one, sometimes-the-other, possibilities' (Oakley, 1992, p. ix). This is a moot point for this discussion of intention, as it may be impossible to impute intention unambiguously and, as will be discussed shortly, it may put other considerations out of range of the considerable.

One challenge to the division between forms of violence on the basis of intention is evidence of similarities in the epidemiology of injuries. This consists in evidence of socio-economic class gradients that pertain for all injuries that arise from unintended or accidental events and, to a lesser extent, intentional or deliberate violence.

People in more deprived socio-economic classes suffer a greater incidence of accidental or unintended violence. This is illustrated by the standardized mortality ratios for children for death by poisonings, motor vehicle accidents, drowning and fire (Botting, 1995). The gradient from a low incidence of deaths in the higher class to the highest incidence of deaths in the lowest class is particularly striking for deaths from fires or flames (Wimbush, 1992; Poyner et al., 1980; Chandler, 1984).

The evidence of a class gradient in intentional injuries is more contentious and less clear cut. There are difficulties in collecting data on physical and sexual assault, particularly within families or households (Hague and Malos, 1993). Statistics referring to the prevalence of violence within the family and between partners are widely assumed to be subject to underreporting. The question of enumerating the non-physical damage of such violence has barely been addressed in attempts to gather statistical evidence. The idea that non-physical after-effects of an assault and/or the fear of as yet uncommitted assault can constitute a form of violence is explored in chapter 2. Women's fears of being assaulted at night on the streets are answered by police advice not to leave home after dark alone. Yet statistically women are more likely to be subjected to assault in their own homes from a partner, relative or acquaintance, and it is young men who are most at risk from violent assault on the street. Thus fear of violence is not straightforwardly related to statistical risk of experiencing it. Arguably the fear of violence that is widespread among certain groups in society is profoundly disabling but in a less easily quantifiable fashion than bodily harm.

Considering only partner battery, rates are somewhat lower for middle class, compared with working class groups, though not low enough to support the view that this form of violence is confined to the lowest socio-economic groups (Kornblit, 1994). The higher rate in lower socio-economic groups may be partly accounted for by disempowered populations being easier to research than those with more power. Data on fear of intentional violence of a variety of types show a strong socio-economic class gradient (Ellaway and Macintyre, 1995).

While the evidence of a social class gradient is less clear for injuries from partner battery than it is for injuries from house fires, the argument here is not that the effect of class on rates of these injuries is identical. Rather, the similarities in the shared class gradients suggest that by considering the two types of violence as categorically different from one another insights into common causal mechanisms are lost. An unexplored area is the possibililty of a mechanism that leads, for instance, to children being vulnerable to violence of all forms under conditions of material deprivation.

The discussion thus far leads to a definition of violence which includes a notion of the power which is defined as the ability to exert physical force on others, and also the ability to appropriate people's symbols and information as well as their territory and economic resources. The exercise of any of these types of power may constitute a form of violence. The definition of violence needs to recognize that power might be unevenly distributed at the inter-personal and the collective level, and that violence might result from both direct and indirect use of force (Agudelo, 1992).

The notion of indirect force is important in this definition, and what it encompasses deserves some discussion. The emphasis on interpersonal intentionality means that indirect violence which involves the exertion of a non-physical force which is not primarily intended to harm is hard to contemplate. A demonstration of the limited utility of intention in analysing the underlying causes of violence is offered by Simon Carter in the last chapter of this volume. Intention is a concept that is so rooted in a model which considers violence to be an interpersonal problem, that it cannot account for the form of violence which Carter describes. Cost-benefit analyses which use economics as a method of trading risks of unlike natures mean that the risk of an 'acceptable' level of 'accidental' violence is allowed for in planning certain scientific and industrial ventures. This type of 'accidental' damage is not only intended, but foreseen and planned for in financial forecasts, and can be viewed as a direct outcome of the application of rationality in risk assessment.

David Stone, in chapter 1, suggests a terminology which avoids assuming there are fundamental differences between intentional and unintentional violence when discussing injuries in the context of public health. For medicine that is involved with remedying physical damage to bodies, the role of intention in causing the hurt is of little account. The lack of utility of centring a definition of violence on intention in the public health of injuries is

5

touched upon by Billie Weiss in chapter 5 when she points out that 'accidental' injuries and homicides from hand guns are a contradiction in terms: the gun is specifically designed to kill and maim, so to call this outcome an accident is misleading. There are parallels between the misnomer of an 'accidental hand gun death' and the euphemisms which surround discussion of fatalities resulting from large scale armed conflicts. For instance, 'friendly fire' is the phrase used when a combatant kills someone who is not constructed as the enemy (see chapter 6), and 'low use segment of the population' is used to refer to people who are considered 'expendable' and can therefore be subject to a high risk of injury or death in nuclear weapons testing (see chapter 7).

Feminist research has made a major contribution towards unravelling the contradictions of violence, and some of this work is discussed in chapters 2 and 3. Feminist understandings of violence have been important in showing how various forms of violence have been, and often still are, defined as socially acceptable. Kate Hunt and Jenny Kitzinger in chapter 3 give a brief historical background to how violence against women and children which has traditionally been hidden or defined as 'natural' and 'inevitable' has now become defined as problematic. The authors' own research shows that violence against women and children is now an issue that the public consider worthy of and suitable for public discussion, rather than a topic that should be avoided.

Chapter 2 by Janette Forman and Jan Macleod shows that there are still aspects of violence that remain unexplored and undiscussed. They demonstrate that the nature of links between different forms of violence (in this case abuse of their partners and children by men) need to be examined because of the way that one form is found to facilitate the other. The method of classifying violence according to its perpetrators by researchers and service providers means that these links are often obscured.

While feminist definitions have worked to delegitimize violence against women and children, there are still marginalized groups who are not fully included in the group of 'innocent' victims of the violence they suffer. The ideology that has seen women to blame when they are sexually assaulted, particularly by men known to them, means that women who are prostitutes are often regarded as more responsible than women who are not sex workers. Soliciting for commercial sex does not, of course, amount to soliciting for sexual violence. Marina Barnard in chapter 4 shows that prostitutes are not treated as blameless victims of violence, and that despite the constraints under which they operate, there are strategies that women adopt to reduce the risk of violence to themselves. A question not explored in this volume is that of the indirect violence done to women who, despite the known increased risks of violent assault, go into prostitution for want of alternative economic options.

Much feminist work, particularly that which is involved in campaigning for change, has focused on redefining men's violence against 'their' women and children as illegitimate, the Zero Tolerance campaign being a prime example. This has meant that the exploration of violence as a social problem, rather than an individual or interpersonal one, has sometimes been neglected.

The last three chapters move away from interpersonal violence to consider how it affects groups of people. Billie Weiss (chapter 5) argues strongly that while 'gang' violence in Los Angeles is confined to particular groups defined by their ethnicity, age and gender, the responsibility for the victims and perpetrators is shared by the whole of society. In the penultimate chapter (6) Anthony Zwi examines the effects of war on individuals and their communities, paying particular attention to the damage that is never enumerated in official statistics about armed conflicts. While in the last fifty years armed conflicts have been eliminated from developed industrial nations, the very regime which has been credited by political leaders with 'keeping the peace' necessitates a level of violence as part of its enterprise. Finally, in chapter 7 Simon Carter expands upon how ventures of the state and of industry in a capitalist society in times of war and peace alike, imply violence towards citizens through the 'rationality' of decision-making processes. Carter's analysis presents a strong challenge to traditional approaches to violence of the legal and medical professions which view progress in understanding the causes of violence in terms of an increasingly rational construction of the problem.

An issue which remains largely unexplored in this volume is the question of when violence might be justified or warranted by the ends it seeks to establish. Nonetheless, included in a definition of violence should be the possibility that people operating under very strong constraints might be faced with violence as their only option.

Bibliography

Agudelo, S.F. (1992), 'Violence and health: preliminary elements for thought and action', *International Journal of Health Services*, Vol. 22, No. 2, pp. 365-76.
Botting, B. (1995), *The Health of Our Children: Decennial Supplement*, OPCS, HMSO, London.
Chandler, S.E., Chapman, A. and Hollington, S.J. (1984), 'Fire incidence, housing and social conditions - the urban situation in Britain', *Fire Prevention*, Vol. 172, pp. 15-26.

Ellaway, A. and Macintyre, S. (1995), *Social Variations in the use of Urban Neighbourhoods*, paper presented at British Sociological Association Annual Conference, April, Leicester.

Hague, G. and Malos, E. (1993), *Domestic Violence. Action for Change*, Cheltenham, New Clarion Press.

Kornblit, A.L. (1994), 'Domestic violence - an emerging health issue' *Social Science and Medicine*, Vol. 39, No. 9, pp. 1181-8.

Oakley, A. (1992), *Social Support and Motherhood*, Blackwell, Oxford.

Poyner, B. (1980), *Personal factors in domestic accidents: Prevention through product and environmental design*, Consumer Safety Unit, Department of Trade, London.

Rosenberg, M.L., O'Carroll, P.W. and Powell, K.E. (1992), 'Let's be clear: violence is a public health problem', *Journal of the American Medical Association*, Vol. 267, No. 22, pp. 3071-2.

Sherwin, S. (1989), 'Philosophical methodology and feminist methodology: are they compatible?', in Garry, A. and Pearsall, M. (ed.s), *Women, Knowledge and Reality*, Unwin Hyman, Boston.

Stanko, E. (1990), *Everyday Violence: How Women And Men Experience Sexual And Physical Danger*, Pandora Press, London.

Wimbush, Erica (1992), *Fatal house fire accidents in Glasgow, 1981-90: Why the excess?*, unpublished MPH dissertation, University of Glasgow, Glasgow.

1 Trauma and its prevention: A public health perspective

David Stone

Introduction

The purpose of this chapter is to provide the reader with an overview of trauma - whether intentional or unintentional - from a public health perspective. Because public health strives to adopt a population based, data driven paradigm, the way trauma is defined and assessed epidemiologically is a major determinant of the approaches used for its control.

Trauma as a public health problem

The nature of trauma The long-standing debate about the relative merits of the terms accident and injury is gradually being resolved in favour of the latter. The title of the First World Conference on Accident and Injury Prevention in 1989 had evolved into the Second World Conference on Injury Control four years later. This is no mere semantic dispute; it relates to the very nature of the phenomena under scrutiny.

These terms are not synonyms. An accident is an event while an injury is a form of pathological state. The former need not always result in the latter. And both may be viewed as occurring in the context of a variety of preceding, accompanying, and subsequent factors any or all of which may influence the ultimate outcome. In other words, the observed injury is the endpoint of a process which comprises a series of events rather than a single occurrence.

An *accident* was originally defined by the World Health Organization as an unpremeditated event resulting in recognizable injury. This proved unsatisfactory for several reasons: it implied an element of randomness and, by inference, unavoidability; it reduced a complex process to a single, notional event; it excluded intentional injury when intent was often difficult or impossible to ascertain; and it failed to take account of covert (i.e. unrecognized or unacknowledged) injury, whether physical or mental.

The modern tendency is to define an *injury* as human damage resulting from acute exposure to physical, chemical or other harmful agent. By dispelling the flavour of randomness, by ignoring the issue of intent and by narrowing the focus on outcome, this definition may be counted a partial success. It too fails, however, to confront the challenge of covert injury.

The term trauma has advantages over either accident or injury since it refers to all forms of damage to humans irrespective of intent, predictability, causation, or outcome. Its current familiarity to clinicians is not yet matched by common usage in the public domain, where trauma and traumatized are more often used in the context of emotional rather than physical distress, but this may change as the concept of post traumatic stress becomes more widely understood.

Whatever terminology is used, the essence of the problem is the deleterious effect on humans of acute exposure to thermal, mechanical, electrical or chemical energy, or from the absence of such essentials as heat or oxygen (NCIPC, 1989). To this might be added the adverse emotional, social, and economic sequels of trauma for victims, their families, peers, and society as a whole. Given the complexity of these processes, the terminological solution adopted here is to retain the term *accident* for the pre-injury events, *injury* for the resulting human damage, and *trauma* for the phenomenon (and all its components) as a whole.

Sources of data on trauma

Trauma data are of two broad types: mortality and morbidity. Mortality data have been most extensively investigated because they are available in most settings, while morbidity data are more problematic to collect. Paradoxically therefore, more is known about the rarer outcomes of injury.

A useful concept is that of the trauma pyramid, with the small number of fatalities at the tip and the much larger number of unreported injuries at the base. Injuries presenting to family doctors, community clinics, and hospitals occupy the centre of the pyramid.

This is not a purely theoretical model. A major study of childhood (0-19 years) injuries in Massachusetts showed that for every death there were 45 hospitalizations and 1300 visits to emergency rooms (Gallagher et al., 1984). An unknown number never reach medical attention.

Mortality data Most developed countries have well established systems for reporting aggregate mortality data abstracted from death certificates. These are usually capable of generating tables showing the numbers, causes, age, sex, and place of residence of the victims. Annual reports on vital statistics are published in the United Kingdom by the Office of Population Censuses and Surveys and the Registrar General for Scotland. These contain valuable information on national and regional patterns of deaths according to broad diagnostic categories (including accidents, poisonings and violence). More detailed tabulations of specific injury causes are published separately for road traffic accidents (Department of Transport, 1991) or are available on request.

The validity of mortality data is variable since they are dependent on the accuracy and completeness of the death certificates from which they derive. In most countries, the issuing of a death certificate is mandatory but the recorded diagnosis is dependent on a range of factors such as clinical skill, the local professional and lay culture, and the medicolegal context.

The major drawback of injury mortality data from the perspective of public health agencies is the lack of causal specificity. A death from a head injury resulting from a road traffic accident may be recorded as a subdural haemorrhage secondary to a fractured skull without any reference to the location, circumstances or mechanism of the injury. One partial solution is to incorporate an additional coding system known as E (external cause) codes into the recording of traumatic death as recommended by the International Classification of Diseases. The uptake of this additional three-digit option has been patchy. E codes are now mandatory for injury mortality coding in parts of the UK and the United States, and there is no doubt that they have enhanced the epidemiological value of routine mortality data substantially.

Morbidity data The usual sources of injury morbidity data are hospital records. These generally take the form of aggregated hospital discharge data containing information on the age and sex of the patient, the diagnosis, and the length of stay. Some contain details of procedures and treatments. All are subject to fairly major limitations.

First, not all hospitals ensure that every hospitalization is recorded on the appropriate form. In Scotland, all hospital discharges are identifiable via the Scottish Morbidity Record system which has operated since the 1960s. In England and Wales, only a 10 per cent sample of discharges were included in the routine monitoring system until the Korner recommendations began to be implemented on a wide scale in the 1990s.

Second, the recorded diagnosis is frequently incomplete or inaccurate. From an administrative point of view, this scarcely matters and is therefore given little attention, while epidemiologically the damage to the data validity can be considerable. In the case of injuries, E coding of hospitalization data is far from universal, although it is mandatory in Scotland and in several US

11

states. A further difficulty lies in the definition of injury for coding purposes. Food poisoning, alcohol intoxication and asbestosis are examples of disorders where ambiguity arises. And the relatively recent recognition of post-traumatic stress disorder means that the psychological effects of a traumatic event are unlikely to be recorded consistently in hospitalization records.

Third, a patient may be admitted more than once for the same injury thereby inflating the true injury incidence. Sophisticated record linkage is required to remove this obstacle to interpretation.

Finally, the decision to hospitalize an injured patient is dependent not only on the clinical state of the patient but on the availability of beds and admission policies. As these non-morbid factors vary, they can introduce biases into incidence data derived from hospitalizations.

Despite these shortcomings, hospital discharge data are extremely important in the assessment of the scale and nature of the injury problem given the dearth of alternative sources of injury morbidity information. Hospital outpatient clinics and accident and emergency departments rarely contribute routine data of any kind although efforts are under way in several places to remedy this.

A multiplicity of other specific databases are held by some specialized units and agencies for research, statutory or other purposes. These include trauma registers, police and fire statistics, and occupational health and safety reporting systems. Even newspaper clippings are a rich source of injury information if systematically scrutinized. All may be subsumed under the generic heading of injury surveillance systems. Depending on the locality and the nature of the injury, these may be invaluable adjuncts to hospitalization data.

The epidemiology of trauma

A glance at a table of the principal causes of mortality in the population aged 1-40 years should persuade the most sceptical reader of the public health importance of trauma. The collective category of 'accidents' is the single largest contributor to deaths in this age group in almost every industrialized country.

In the UK, injuries cause about 12,000 deaths each year, or two-thirds of all deaths of healthy people. This accounts for 8 per cent of all potential years of life lost under 75 years (Department of Health, 1993). While the proportion of deaths due to trauma is highest in the younger age groups, the absolute number of deaths is highest in the elderly. Over the past 30 years, there appears to have been a downward trend in trauma mortality (which may now have reached a plateau) but this should be viewed in the context of a declining death rate generally. The UK has one of the lowest death rates from injuries (particularly related to road accidents) in Europe with the exception of pedestrian rates, especially for children.

There are wide regional variations in trauma mortality within the UK. Scotland has a poorer record than England and Wales for reasons which are obscure (Scottish Office, 1992) but which may relate to a greater concentration of social disadvantage or to higher rates of cigarette and possibly alcohol consumption. In relative terms, the main problems in Scotland appear to be child pedestrian injuries and domestic fires.

The epidemiology of injuries varies with severity (Walsh and Jarvis, 1992). While road accidents contribute the largest proportion of deaths, home accidents contribute the largest proportion of hospital admissions. The social class gradient in injury rates is more pronounced in fatal than in non-fatal injuries, at least in children.

Fortunately, most injuries have non-fatal consequences. In the UK, they lead to about half a million hospital admissions (8 per cent of the total) each year, and about 7 million attendances (almost half the total) at accident and emergency departments (NAHA/RoSPA, 1990). An unknown but undoubtedly large number of injured people are treated by community health services, including primary care, or do not present to any agency.

The causes of trauma

The main causes of injury in the population are accidents on the road, in the home and during leisure or sporting activities. Their relative contributions vary according to age group: young children and the elderly tend to be injured in the home while older children and adults tend to be injured on the roads, at work or during play. Other important causes include poisonings, assaults and medical mishaps. Some of these will be discussed in more detail.

Home injuries Children and the elderly are most at risk from injuries sustained in the home. Pre-school children are at particular risk partly because of their greater exposure to household hazards and partly because of their developmental stage.

According to the Home Accident Surveillance System (HASS), home accidents account for about 40 per cent of all fatal accidents and a third of all injuries treated in UK hospitals (Department of Trade and Industry, 1992). The most severe home injuries in childhood are associated with fires, burns and scalds, falls, poisonings and drownings (Towner et al., 1993). Boys are at greater risk of death than girls and social disadvantage is an important risk factor (Alwash and McCarthy, 1988).

13

Most home injuries in the elderly are due to falls. These may be precipitated either by intrinsic or environmental factors and identifying the relative importance of each may be difficult. It seems that with advancing age, postural sway and drop attacks are more likely to cause a fall than environmental hazards (Livesley, 1984).

Road injuries Road traffic accidents are the major cause of accidental death in children under 15 and in young adults. Of the 300,000 injury accidents reported each year in Britain through the police, about 80 per cent are slight, 18 per cent serious and under 2 per cent fatal (Department of Transport, 1991). Fatal and serious casualty rates are higher in Scotland than in England and Wales, particularly in the case of child pedestrians (Scottish Development Department, 1989).

Concern about child pedestrians has prompted several investigations. Children run more than double the risk of being a pedestrian casualty than adults (Ward, 1991). Young children tend to be injured on local roads near their homes while older children and adults tend to be injured on main roads. The children most at risk are 11-14 years and there may have been a rise in casualty rates in this group (Preston, 1989).

Leisure injuries Data on leisure injuries are more elusive than those occurring in homes or on the roads. The UK Leisure Accident Surveillance System draws information from hospitals around the country (Department of Trade and Industry, 1992) and is linked to the HASS. Most of the available information relating to causes concerns children at play, at school or participating in sport. Important causes of serious leisure injuries include water immersion (Kemp and Sibert, 1992), playground accidents (Ball and King, 1991), and rugby football.

Interpersonal violence Violence is rarely seen as a public health problem (Shepherd and Farrington, 1993). This is extraordinary when one considers that assault has become the leading cause of death in some sectors of the population. In 1985 in the US, interpersonal violence caused about 50,000 deaths and a quarter of a million hospital admissions. Those most at risk tend to be inner city dwelling, poor, young, and black (see chapter 5). One in 12 young black American males is a victim of violent crime each year (Langan and Innes, 1985).

Traditionally, violence and its control have been the province of criminologists and the judiciary respectively. However, their attention has tended to focus on the perpetrator rather than on the victims because of their preoccupation with the attribution of blame. Public health can adopt a broader perspective whereby all of the causal factors, along with the range of outcomes (whether or not the result of criminal intent), can be examined and acted upon (Rosenberg and Fenley, 1991). In this sense, a public health approach to violence transcends legalistic definitions of intent and consequences.

Rates of violence derived from police statistics can be highly misleading because of variations in reporting. In England and Wales for example, police statistics showed a 40 per cent increase in the number of woundings between 1981 and 1987 while the British Crime Survey revealed an increase of only 12 per cent. Moreover, there appears to be substantial underreporting to the police of assaults (particularly those committed in a domestic setting where women and children are the principal victims (see chapter 2) if these are compared with attendances at hospital accident and emergency departments (Shepherd et al., 1990).

Alcohol and drug abuse are established risk factors for interpersonal violence - in both perpetrators and victims - although their precise causal significance is unknown (Shepherd 1990). There is some evidence that addictive behaviour is less a cause of violent crime than an accompaniment of it, or a marker of deviant behaviour generally (Hammersley et al., 1990). Other potential risk factors include consumption of psychotropic drugs, impulsive personality types and (controversially) exposure to media violence. Studies of violent offenders have shown that they tend to have low intelligence, to have a history of behaviour disorders in childhood, to have come from families with disharmonious parents and to have experienced harsh and erratic discipline (Farrington, 1991). These data should be treated with caution. The majority of studies of violent behaviour are retrospective and lack adequate control groups for comparison. The few prospective studies are fraught with methodological and interpretative problems including a tendency to ignore potentially confounding socio-economic variables.

The consequences of trauma

The economic burden to the community of trauma is enormous (Stone, 1993). The total annual costs of childhood injuries in England and Wales amount to around £200 million and of injuries in all age groups to about £30 billion, of which about £1 billion are health service costs.

More important than the economic costs of trauma are the direct and indirect effects on the quality of life of victims and their families. These sequelae include emotional and social as well as physical effects and fall under two headings: disability, and post-traumatic stress disorder.

Information on the long term effects of injuries and the disability associated with them is sparse, although a number of studies have addressed this aspect of road accidents, especially those involving head injury (Research Institute for Consumer Affairs, 1980). Some data on disability following injuries are available from the General Household Survey.

The growing recognition of post-traumatic stress disorder introduces another potentially adverse outcome - of non-injury accidents as well as injuries - into the equation. The paucity of routine data on this outcome severely limits attempts to establish a comprehensive profile of the consequences of trauma in the population.

Trauma prevention and public health

Prevention in relation to the natural history of trauma

Traumatic injury is less an event than a process. In this sense, trauma can be said to have a natural history analogous to other pathological processes. At one end of the natural history is health, at the other, death. The particular outcome of a traumatic process is dependent on the interaction of a series of factors operating along this dynamic continuum.

The concept of trauma as a process is relatively recent. An early formulation was that of Haddon (1972) who devised a so-called injury matrix comprising three phases - pre-injury, injury, and post-injury - interacting with three categories of factors. This matrix is strongly reminiscent of the host, agent and environment triad of classical epidemiology (see Table 1.1).

Haddon's matrix is narrowly focused on the period around the time of the injury itself, but the principle is a useful one and can be extended to include earlier and later phases in the natural history. Moreover, the matrix is not merely a theoretical construct - it carries profound implications for prevention. In turn, this may be regarded as operating at three levels: primary, secondary and tertiary. The categories are not mutually exclusive and indeed may all be involved in a given preventive response. Conceptually, each preventive level exactly parallels each phase of the natural history.

Primary prevention of trauma

Primary prevention seeks to intervene in the natural history in the pre-injury phase - that is, to pre-empt the occurrence of the injury by interrupting the chain of events leading to it. In the example given to illustrate the Haddon matrix, primary prevention would aim to reduce alcohol intoxication, the carrying of lethal weapons, and drug dealing. Achieving these objectives requires the deployment of a combination of strategies often described as the three 'E's - education, engineering, and enforcement.

The same principles can be applied to the primary prevention of interpersonal violence. Firearms are responsible for over half of all violent deaths

16

in the United States. Controlling the number of firearms in circulation and limiting the access of the population to lethal weaponry are amongst the measures which have been advocated by anti-violence campaigners (NCIPC, 1989; Weiss, this volume).

Table 1.1
Haddon's Matrix (modified by the author): The example of a fatal injury to the chest caused by a knife attack

Phase	Factors		
	Host	Agent	Environment
Pre-injury	Alcohol intoxication	Carrying knife	Drug dealing
Injury	Vulnerable to assault	Knife used to inflict wound	Passive bystanders
Post-injury	Haemorrhage from major vessel	Attacker removes knife and flees	Inadequate emergency medical care

Source: adapted from Haddon, 1972

Secondary prevention of trauma

Secondary prevention does not aspire to modify the pre-injury phase of the natural history, but rather to ensure that the energy transfer is rapidly dissipated in such a way as to avoid or minimize pathological effects on the victim. Restricting the availability of exceptionally lethal knives, for example, might ameliorate the consequences of an assault without in any way affecting the event itself.

Another example of secondary prevention is the fitting of smoke detectors. These cannot prevent fires, but they can alert the occupants of a building to a fire and thereby pre-empt injury or death. Similarly, the wearing of car seat belts can minimize the extent of injury to the occupants while not preventing the accident itself.

The secondary prevention of firearm injuries aims to limit the occurrence or severity of injuries resulting from violent assaults. This can be achieved by

17

passing and enforcing strict regulations on the nature of available weapons and their ammunition.

Tertiary prevention of trauma

Tertiary prevention seeks to minimize the harmful consequences of injuries rather than to prevent their occurrence. Rapid and effective first aid - to stop haemorrhage, for example - is a form of immediate post-injury tertiary prevention. The physical, mental, and social rehabilitation of injury victims requires a much longer time scale but is nevertheless an equally important means of tertiary prevention.

Both victims and perpetrators of violence have been targets of tertiary prevention programmes, particularly in the United States. Apart from the spectrum of health and other agencies involved in this area, mutual support groups can offer a range of follow-up services and information to victims and these appear to have been highly successful. Counselling services, youth clubs and a variety of community-based initiatives have attempted to prevent recidivism among offenders with varying results. Skilled professional assessment and management of patients presenting to hospital with any form of injury, whether or not intentional, is an aspect of health care which has been neglected to date.

Obstacles to prevention

The implementation of effective injury prevention programmes is fraught with difficulties. Some of these are organizational, technical or financial. More often, they have roots in negative or hostile attitudes, lack of data, and a shortage of professional skills.

The major obstacles to injury prevention may be summarised by the three 'I's - ignorance, ineffectiveness and indifference.

Ignorance of the scale and the potential for avoiding injuries is widespread. This is compounded by a lack of high quality data on injury frequency and causation. (By contrast, there is no *quantitative* shortage of injury data in most industrialized countries). In addition, evaluation studies of preventive interventions are relatively rare.

Those interventions which have been evaluated have frequently been found to be *ineffective*. Huge resources have been squandered for example, on exclusively or predominantly educational approaches to safety which have made little or no impact on injury incidence.

Indifference on the part of policy makers and the public partly reflects the influence of the two factors described above, and is partly the result of successful lobbying by vested interests opposed to measures (such as gun control in the US) which threaten their economic viability.

In clinical practice, it is axiomatic that diagnosis should precede treatment. By analogy, public health practice requires that community diagnosis should precede preventive interventions targeted at the population. Extending the analogy further, once the treatment has been prescribed, the clinician will reassess the patient after a period of time and may be obliged to revise the diagnosis; the public health physician will do likewise at a population level.

While there is no paucity of injury mortality data to facilitate the task of community diagnosis, morbidity data are much more limited in availability and scope. Health service morbidity data are mainly confined to hospitalizations. There have been sporadic attempts to extend routine data collection to accident and emergency departments since most moderately or severely injured people will pass through their doors.

By establishing so-called injury surveillance systems, health authorities and other agencies have striven to fulfil their need to assess the incidence and causes of injuries (other than deaths) in the population since this is the only rational means of planning and evaluating preventive interventions. Examples of such systems include the US SCIPP (Statewide Child Injury Prevention Program), CHIRPP (Canadian Hospitals Injury Reporting and Prevention Program) and the Australian VISS (Victorian Injury Surveillance System). UK schemes operating outside the health service include the industrial RIDDOR (Reporting of Injuries, Diseases and Dangerous Occurrences Regulations) system and the *Stats 19* used by the police.

Evaluating preventive measures

When a preventive action has been taken, its beneficial effect cannot be taken for granted. Large-scale educational campaigns for example, were once the mainstay of public health policies to reduce injury rates. However, carefully designed research studies have tended to show the futility of exclusively educational approaches to safety promotion (Towner et al., 1993).

Without evaluation, the public health task is incomplete. This is now a widely accepted view. Controversy arises however, when specific evaluation methods are proposed. Academic researchers argue for rigorously designed controlled experiments which are simply not feasible in many situations. The more pragmatic approaches include before-and-after comparisons which are easily dismissed on purist methodological grounds. How can the dilemma be resolved?

In a sense, the purist-pragmatic dichotomy is a false one, arising in part from a semantic confusion. If there is strong research evidence that a particular intervention works, there is no need to repeat the original study every time it is applied in practice. In other words, its *efficacy* has already been established even if its local *effectiveness* has not. More rigorous methodological standards are required to assess the former than the latter. The confusion arises because the term *evaluation* is applied to both. And while the randomized controlled trial is the most powerful experimental tool for evaluating efficacy, a range of alternative options are available to evaluate effectiveness. These include before-and-after comparisons, and the systems approach of Donabedian (1966) based on a review of structure, process, and outcome.

There are two fundamental features of all forms of evaluation. First, they are dependent on a comparison of some kind - against a control group for example, or a set of objectives. Without the comparative dimension, any information collected cannot be subjected to an evaluative interpretation. Second, they require data, quantitative or qualitative (or preferably both).

Towards a trauma prevention strategy

Why do we need a strategy?

Although an abstract entity, a strategy does not exist in an intellectual or an organizational vacuum. Its purpose is to promote the achievement of a goal or series of goals. Moreover, its strength lies in its component parts without which it is devoid of meaning.

A strategy has two main advantages over an *ad hoc* or piecemeal approach. First, it ensures that a goal is addressed systematically and efficiently - that is, without gaps or duplication. Second, it sets out priorities. These are vital in an era in which all new resource allocation is subjected to critical scrutiny.

Levels of strategy setting - international, national and local

The various geographical and administrative levels at which injury prevention strategies have been devised are to a large extent interrelated.

In 1978, the Alma Ata Declaration of the World Health Organization led to the development of further international statements on the need to achieve 'health for all' by the year 2000. In turn, the various regions of the WHO articulated specified targets for the achievement of this global objective. By the mid-1980s, the British government (among others) had become a signatory to the European HFA 2000 strategy which included mortality targets for a range of disorders including accidents.

Several years later, these international efforts were translated into UK national policy statements, most notably 'The Health of the Nation'

(Department of Health, 1992) for England. This identified five key health promotion areas to which were attached population targets. The accident targets were:

1. to reduce road casualties by 30 per cent by the year 2000 (from a baseline of the 1980-85 average).
2. to reduce the death rate for accidents in
     a. children under 15 by at least 33 per cent
     b. young people (15-24) by at least 25 per cent
     c. older people (65 and over) by at least 33 per cent by the year 2005 (from a 1990 baseline).

No local targets were specified, but a number of regions and districts have since set their own targets broadly in line with the national ones.

Components of a model trauma prevention strategy - objectives, programmes, performance targets, resources

The Health of the Nation initiative has been criticized on several grounds. First, it appears unduly preoccupied with targets, many of which are unrealistic or easily attainable without any further action. Second, the five key areas do not cover the entire range of health problems suffered by the population and cannot therefore be regarded as sufficiently comprehensive to merit the 'health of the nation' descriptor. Third, no new resources have been allocated to the exercise.

An ideal or model trauma prevention strategy for a nation would comprise:

1. a stated aim
2. specific objectives listed in order of priority
3. a series of thematic programmes
4. explicit programme-specific performance targets
5. anticipated resource requirements over defined time periods.

The British strategy papers represent a useful starting point, but more detailed strategic development is essential if momentum is to be maintained.

Trauma prevention - whose responsibility?

The current position in the UK - who does what?

There is no single agency in the UK which has responsibility for injury prevention. The Health of the Nation Key Area Handbook on Accidents

(Department of Health, 1993) lists seven national organizations with a special interest in accident prevention. This is reflected in an even larger number of injury data sources: in Scotland, 19 sources were listed in a recent review (Scottish Office Interdepartmental Working Party on Accidents, 1994).

Although statutory responsibilities for safety are well defined, the absence of a single lead agency for the overall monitoring and prevention of injuries results in substantial overlapping of interests and data. It also causes enormous practical problems for research workers and others who seek to obtain an overview of the entire injury field. More importantly, the development of an integrated injury prevention strategy is virtually impossible. The example of the US, where a national Division of Injury Control was established under the auspices of the Center for Disease Control in Atlanta, is one which the UK might wish to emulate.

The role of the National Health Service and public health departments

Trauma is without doubt a major public health problem (Pless, 1991) and as such should be a prime responsibility of the National Health Service (NHS). A role for the NHS which goes beyond treatment is gradually becoming acknowledged, but there are difficulties in defining a specifically health service contribution to a phenomenon which has its roots in the home, on the roads, at work, and in other areas outwith the remit of conventional health care.

Recognising that most injury prevention measures are best applied in non-NHS settings, the role of the health service in promoting safety is probably largely confined to two activities: advocacy, and information gathering. The former can be achieved by the Director of Public Health using the public platform of the Annual Report. The latter is best pursued by collating the wide range of routine data on injuries resulting in death or hospitalization, and by encouraging the development of local injury surveillance systems based in Accident and Emergency departments.

The role of academic departments

The effective application of injury prevention measures is dependent on the fulfilment of the public health tasks of community diagnosis, the selection of appropriate preventive interventions, and evaluation. Research workers can contribute to all three by conducting descriptive and analytical studies, by reviewing the literature and by performing evaluations. The research agenda will, however, have to respond more explicitly to these service tasks if academic departments and research centres are to make a substantive contribution to solving the injury problem.

No panacea exists to eradicate injuries in the population. The current lack of a serious and integrated public health effort with adequate resources to confront the important issues is seriously jeopardising the prospects for progress.

Nevertheless, action is already under way across a broad front. To maintain momentum, the following five steps would be helpful:

1. to recognize that injuries are caused by a range of underlying and often complex factors including random events and interpersonal assault, and can lead to a wide range of physical, emotional and social outcomes;

2. to develop a comprehensive strategy for trauma prevention which incorporates the phenomenon in all its forms including suicide and violence;

3. to establish a single overarching agency with responsibility for co-ordinating trauma surveillance and prevention nationally;

4. to link research explicitly with service needs;

5. to allocate resources to trauma prevention, research and education commensurate with the scale of the problem in the population.

Bibliography

Alwash, R. and McCarthy, M. (1988), 'Accidents in the home among children under 5: ethnic differences or social disadvantage?', *British Medical Journal*, Vol. 296, p. 1450.

Ball, D.J. and King, K.L. (1991), 'Playground injuries: a scientific appraisal of popular concerns', *Journal of the Royal Society of Health*, Vol. 3, pp. 134-7.

Department of Health. (1992), *The Health of the Nation - A Strategy for Health in England*, Cm 1986, Department of Health, London.

Department of Health. (1993), *The Health of the Nation Key Area Handbook - Accidents*, Department of Health, London.

Department of Trade and Industry, Consumer Safety Unit. (1992), *Home and Leisure Accident Research*, Department of Trade and Industry, London.

Department of Transport. (1991), *Road Accidents Great Britain 1990 (The Casualty Report)*, HMSO, London.

Donabedian, A. (1966), 'Evaluating the quality of medical care', *Millbank Memorial Fund Quarterly*, Vol. 44, pp. 166-203.

Farrington, D.P. (1991), 'Childhood aggression and adult violence: early precursors and later-life outcomes' in Pegler, D.J. and Rubin, K.H. (eds.), *The Development and Treatment of Childhood Aggression*, Erlbaum, Hillsdale, NJ.

Gallagher, S.S., Finison, K., Guyer, B. and Goodenough, S. (1984), 'The incidence of injuries among 87,000 Massachusetts children and adolescents: results of the 1980-81 Statewide Childhood Injury Prevention Program Surveillance System', *American Journal of Public Health*, Vol. 74, pp. 340-7.

Haddon, W. (1972), 'A logical framework for categorising highway safety phenomena and activity', *Journal of Trauma*, Vol. 12, pp. 197-207.

Hammersley, R., Forsyth, A. and Lavelle, T. (1990), 'The criminality of new drug users in Glasgow', *British Journal of Addiction*, Vol. 85, pp. 1583-94.

Kemp, A.M. and Sibert, J.R. (1992), 'Drowning and near drowning in children in the United Kingdom: lessons for prevention', *British Medical Journal*, Vol. 304, pp. 1143-6.

Langan, P.A. and Innes, C.A. (1985), *The Risk of Violent Crime*, Bureau of Justice Statistics, Washington, DC.

Livesley, B. (1984), 'Falls in older age', *British Medical Journal*, Vol. 289, pp. 568-9.

National Association of Health Authorities/Royal Society for the Prevention of Accidents. (1990), *Action on Accidents - the Unique Role of the Health Service*, NAHA, Birmingham.

National Committee for Injury Prevention and Control. (1989), *Injury Prevention: Meeting the Challenge*, Oxford University Press, New York.

Pless, I.B. (1991), 'Accident prevention', *British Medical Journal*, Vol. 303, pp. 462-4.

Preston, B. (1989), 'Child pedestrian casualties with special reference to casualties on the journey to or from school in Manchester and Salford, England', *Accident Analysis and Prevention*, Vol. 21, pp. 291-7.

Research Institute for Consumer Affairs. (1980), *Knocked Down. A study of the personal and family consequences of road accidents involving pedestrians and pedal cyclists*, Consumer Association, London.

Scottish Development Department/ MVA Consultancy. (1989), *'Must Do Better'. A study of child pedestrian accidents and road crossing behaviour in Scotland*, Scottish Office, Edinburgh.

Scottish Office. (1992), *Scotland's Health - A Challenge To Us All*, HMSO, Edinburgh.

Scottish Office Interdepartmental Working Party on Accidents. (1994), *Scottish Accident Statistics 1980-91*, Scottish Office Home and Health Department, Edinburgh.

Shepherd, J.P. (1990), 'Alcohol and violence', *Lancet*, Vol. 335, p. 796.

Shepherd, J.P. and Farrington, D.P. (1993), 'Assault as a public health problem: discussion paper', *Journal of the Royal Society of Medicine*, Vol. 86, pp. 89-92.

Shepherd, J.P., Shapland, M., Pearce, N.X. and Scully, C. (1990), 'Pattern, severity and aetiology of injuries in victims of assault', *Journal of the Royal Society of Medicine*, Vol. 83, pp. 75-8.

Rosenberg, M.L. and Fenley, M.A. (eds.), (1991), *Violence in America: A Public Health Approach*, Oxford University Press, New York.

Stone, D.H. (1993), 'Costs and benefits of accident prevention' in Popay, J. and Young, A. (eds.), *Reducing Accidental Death and Injury in Children*, Public Health Research and Resource Centre/Manchester Public Health Resource Centre, Manchester.

Towner, E., Dowswell, T. and Jarvis, S. (1993), *Reducing childhood accidents. The effectiveness of health promotion interventions: a literature review*, Health Education Authority, London.

Ward, H. (1991), *Preventing Road Accidents to Children: The Role of the NHS*. Health Education Authority, London.

Walsh, S.S., and Jarvis, S.N. (1992), 'Measuring the frequency of 'severe' accidental injury in childhood', *Journal of Epidemiology and Community Health*, Vol. 46, pp. 26-32.

2 Working against violence against women and children

Janette Forman and Jan Macleod

Background

In Scotland, the vast majority of specific services for abused women are provided through the voluntary sector, largely by women's organizations working with a feminist analysis of male violence. The main area of work for these groups (for example, Women's Aid groups and Rape Crisis Centres) involves offering a service for individual women. These organizations are heavily worked and under-resourced.

From 1983 to 1993, the numbers of abused women per year contacting Women's Aid in Scotland increased from 8,777 to 22,641; these statistics indicate that the demand on services is high (S.W.A., 1993). Scottish Women's Aid's 289 refuge spaces leave Women's Aid groups far short of the 733 spaces recommended in a report published in 1991 by the Convention of Scottish Local Authorities (C.O.S.L.A., 1991). Rape Crisis Centres are also overwhelmed with requests for support from individual women. In 1992-93 Strathclyde Rape Crisis Centre received almost 3,000 calls (S.R.C., 1993).

As well as dealing with the volume of work involved in offering support to individual women, feminist voluntary organisations work to raise public awareness of male violence, and to campaign on a wide range of issues. However, there are tensions in balancing individual support work, often in a crisis situation, with longer term development and education work.

These tensions were in evidence in Strathclyde Rape Crisis in the early 1980s. The Rape Crisis Centre was receiving an increasing number of calls from abused women, particularly in relation to childhood sexual abuse. At the same time workers from a range of other services such as social work, health, education, police and the legal system, were requesting information on how they could improve their services to abused women. Since the Centre prioritized direct support to abused women, it was extremely difficult to respond effectively to the need for support and information for workers in other organisations.

The Women's Support Project was set up to meet this need. Two of the aims were to bridge the gap between statutory organizations and feminist voluntary organizations and to develop ways of communicating the expertise of feminist organizations in supporting abused women.

The Women's Support Project was opened in 1983 as a voluntary organization based in the east end of Glasgow and now employs four workers: two development workers, and two information workers. The Project is managed by a voluntary Management Committee made up of women with skills and experience in similar areas of work. Core funding now comes from Strathclyde Regional Council.

The Women's Support Project does not offer a long term counselling service, but instead concentrates on education, developing ways of working, providing resources, and encouraging an inter-agency approach. Since we do not offer individual support in the form of counselling, we have developed an information service and Resource Library in order to offer something to individual abused women. This library is now well used by abused women, family and friends, and workers who are in turn supporting abused women. It has proved to be an invaluable resource which allows women access to information which is often not available elsewhere.

Our training workshops on male violence bring together workers from statutory and voluntary organizations and interested individuals. We aim to raise awareness, challenge attitudes, increase confidence in working with abused women and provide access to resources. We organize support groups for women, for example for women abused as children and for women whose children have been sexually abused. We also offer support to women through self-defence and personal safety courses which aim to provide a safe environment where women can discuss experiences and fears of violence. People supporting abused women and children often need support for themselves, we therefore offer them a consultancy service. We have carried out research to highlight the extent of violence against women and the links with other forms of violence - for example a survey into the extent of violence, and research on links between domestic violence and child sexual abuse.

A common root: links between different forms of male violence

Since the Women's Support Project developed out of the work of the Rape Crisis Centre, it was initially identified mainly with rape and sexual assault. As we began to develop our work with the local community, and to meet with statutory organizations, we realized that it was not helpful to abused women, or people supporting them, to continue working on a single issue.

Male violence affects women's lives in many complex and overlapping ways. When we talk of abused women there is a tendency to assume a woman has been abused in one way only, for example she has been raped, or she has suffered domestic violence, or she has been abused as a child. When a woman seeks support or information the possibility that she may have been abused in more than one way, or by more than one person, whether at the same time or at different points in her life, may not always be initially considered by friends, family, or by service providers. Research into women's daily experience shows that this is far from the truth. Highlighting the complex ways in which male violence affects women's lives, Kelly writes:

> As I transcribed and analysed the interviews, it became clear that most women had experienced sexual violence in their lives. It was also clear that the range of men's behaviour that women defined as abusive was neither reflected in legal codes nor in the analytic categories used in previous research. In order to reflect this complexity I began to use the term 'continuum' to describe both the extent and the range of sexual violence recorded in the interviews ... Many women found it helpful in understanding both their own experience and sexual violence in general (Kelly, 1988 p.74).

Feminist organizations have played an important part in the process of naming the violence that women have suffered and publicly naming it as abuse. Women's Aid have been successful in increasing public understanding of abuse in the home, so that, for example, there is a greater awareness that such violence includes mental cruelty and sexual abuse as well as physical violence. However, to change attitudes is a slow process, and all too often women fear that the abuse they have suffered will not be seen by others as 'real' violence. Rape Crisis Centres, by their name alone, have identified rape as a major problem in our society: the term 'crisis' applying not only to individual women, but to the effect of rape and the fear of rape on all women's lives. While this has been an important step, there is still a long way to go. Despite the existence of Rape Crisis for over twenty years, the majority of rapes still go unreported to the authorities.

Although women's organizations usually publicize themselves around a single form of violence, in practice they will offer support to women who have been abused in other situations. Many Women's Aid groups offer support to women abused as children. However, for women who have not yet made contact, there can be a dilemma as to which is the most appropriate organization. If you have been raped by your partner, should you go to Women's Aid or Rape Crisis Centre? If you have been abused as a child, and sexually assaulted as an adult do you need to approach two different organizations for support? More importantly, there is a danger that this situation unintentionally reinforces the assumption that it is rare for women to be abused more than once.

Dealing with each form of violence separately is not helpful when it comes to reviewing or planning services for abused women. At training sessions on child sexual abuse we find that it is common for workers' analyses of a situation involving child sexual abuse to be 'stuck' at the stage of blaming the child's mother, rather than placing responsibility with the abuser. This is particularly likely to happen when the abuser is the mother's partner. 'She must have known' is a common attitude which can prevent workers from moving on to put responsibility with the person who carried out the abuse.

In order to challenge this attitude we find that it is helpful to begin training sessions with discussion on power relationships in the family. Scottish Women's Aid have developed a group exercise which looks at women's experiences of violence in the home (S.W.A., 1993, p.44). This examines in detail the possible extent and effect of domestic violence and aims to give workers an understanding of the process involved in such abuse. This enables workers to consider the extent to which male violence in the home is legitimated by society, for example through the failure of police and courts to protect women. It also establishes a broader context for understanding the abuse of children in the home.

Due to the inter-related nature of violence against women the Women's Support Project expanded its publicized service to cover all areas of male violence, and a main aim of the work has been to highlight links between different forms of violence. This has been clearly stated in our publicity materials. We find that this can make it easier for women to approach the Project for support, with less worry for them that they are contacting the 'wrong' organization. There is no doubt that this worry is a factor for women considering approaching organizations for help. Many phone calls to the Project begin with 'I'm not sure if I am phoning the right place but I didn't know who else to phone'. Similarly some women are surprised to learn that they can approach Women's Aid for support following emotional and sexual abuse in a relationship, a common response being 'I thought that they were only for battered women'. Historically, domestic violence has been portrayed as a woman with a bruised face, when in fact many women suffer abuse and have no visible signs of bruising.

As well as the embarrassment or shame which can be attached to having to tell of abuse that has been suffered, for some women there are fears about losing care of their children. An 'open door' approach allows women an opportunity to gather information which, in turn, can open up other sources of support.

Making links between different forms of male violence has been an invaluable approach in training, providing workers with a framework which allows them to begin to make sense of the day to day violence suffered by women.

Abuse as a continuum

The Project works to increase understanding of the extent and effects of abuse, including how one form of abuse can be facilitated, or the effects compounded, by other forms of male violence. For example pornography is sometimes used to facilitate the sexual abuse of children. Not only can this be used to persuade children that the abuser's behaviour is justified, 'other children do it too', but it can increase the child's sense of powerlessness, 'there is no point in complaining since adults are allowed to do this with children'. Furthermore, pornography can be used to degrade the mother and to show the child that she too is in a powerless position.

In 1989 the Project organized a survey on the extent of violence suffered by women (Bell and Macleod, 1989). This was carried out in conjunction with a local evening newspaper. The paper ran articles on male violence over three days, and on the fourth day printed a one page questionnaire which women readers were invited to complete and return. One thousand, five hundred and three women completed the questionnaire. We anticipated that women might want to expand on some of the points raised in the questionnaire so we asked women for permission to quote from any additional information they chose to include. In the event nearly 300 women wrote letters detailing abuse they had suffered and the vast majority gave permission for this information to be quoted. These women's comments demonstrated the range of violent acts suffered by women and the fact that this violence should be seen as a continuum, rather than a series of unrelated incidents.

Focusing on severe assaults, such as rape, perpetuates the myth that male violence is a problem that only affects a small minority of women. When women are asked about the range of assaults they have experienced, including being followed, flashed at, receiving obscene phone calls and sexual harassment, a picture emerges of widespread everyday intimidation of women which creates in them a high level of fear for their safety.

It is not generally acknowledged that all women live with a high level of male violence and harassment. The problem is constantly dismissed, minimized and distorted. So called 'minor' assaults such as being flashed at or receiving obscene phone calls are often seen as unimportant and even amusing. After the event it may be possible to describe such incidents as amusing, but at the time women do not know how the incident will end. It is a reminder to women of the ever present threat of male violence.

The extent to which actual violence and fear of violence limits women's lives can be highlighted by looking at individual experiences. When a number of examples are studied together a picture of the complex effects of day to day violence begins to emerge. The following quotes are taken from letters sent to the Project along with the survey forms and are grouped together to highlight some of the main issues emerging from the survey.

How fear limits women's freedom

A number of women wrote to express their feelings about how concern for their safety places limits on their freedom. The following examples illustrate the amount of time and energy that women use to plan their daily activities in an effort to avoid dangerous situations:

> If I am alone my chain goes on my door and I always look through my spyhole before opening my door even during the day. Dreadful to have to live like this. I watch where I go during the day time if I am by myself, if someone is with me I am alright. I just never go out at night. I am too afraid to go in the dark alone. If I must go out for some reason which isn't often, my husband goes with me or I get a taxi. I am in every night during winter.

> I wouldn't take a country walk alone etc, my husband can without thinking twice but I don't think a woman can.

> Although I have never been followed by a man/men, I am certain that the reason for this is simply that I would not go out alone at night.

In spite of the limitations that women impose on their own behaviour, time and time again we hear police asking women to further limit their freedom in

32

the wake of the latest publicized attack. This raises a question about the effectiveness of safety campaigns which focus on women's behaviour rather than challenging male violence. It seems clear that women are already highly conscious of their safety, and furthermore, that women are angry about the ways in which the danger of male violence limits their freedom of movement and their leisure and employment opportunities. In this climate, advice from the police often seems patronizing and serves only to reinforce the idea that women are responsible for avoiding violence and divert attention from men's role in carrying out the violence.

Comments from women also demonstrated how an incident can have long lasting effects, although no physical assault may have taken place, and the incident might barely amount to a crime in the eyes of the law:

> I am angry that I now feel afraid whenever I take my short cut home
> ... after I was followed one Sunday morning after church. I can never
> forget the feeling of fear inside me wondering how it was going to
> end and although no assault took place it has left me feeling very
> uneasy whenever I'm out alone. I'll always remember the shuffling of
> his shoes, as he kept in step with my steps and I shall never forget his
> face grinning at me as he became aware of my fear ... Men who do
> this for 'kicks' or 'a laugh' must also be considered dangerous and a
> threat to women. They take away our independence and our freedom
> and ruin our trust in all men.

Obscene phone calls are another area of abuse which is often dismissed as 'harmless'. Fortunately, changes in the telephone system, and cooperation between British Telecom and the police, now mean that it is considerably easier to catch persistent offenders. However, this does little to lessen the shock such a call can bring. As with most areas of male violence, research reveals that the majority of obscene calls are made by men known to the victim. This is one further technique by which abusive men can threaten partners and ex-partners.

> I did many years ago receive filthy calls, I reported it to the police,
> the first thing I was asked - are you married - no divorced - he just
> laughed and said it was probably an old boyfriend ... I was frantic.
> This went on for some time ... for many weeks I was frightened to go
> to sleep.

As the policeman referred to in this letter indicates, obscene calls can be part of harassment from ex-husbands and ex-boyfriends. In this woman's case, as in other cases, we see that the police are aware of the realities of women being terrorized by men known to them but consider this to be less serious than abuse from strangers. The following quote illustrates how abusive phone calls can become much more threatening if the recipient has previous experience of other forms of violence from the perpetrator:

> [My ex-husband] never hit me, but shouts, swears, threatens to kill me, kill my baby, kill himself, kill us all. He phones continually and is very abusive ... I'm frightened to put the phone down on him in case he comes round - at least I know where he is.

This letter highlights the stark choice which can face women, that is having to put up with one form of abuse in order to try to avoid other forms of abuse which are more dangerous or more frightening. In a similar fashion, women who suffer violence at home are often forced to stay in or return to an abusive domestic situation because of fears or experiences of violence outside their home. For instance, women have been sexually assaulted and harassed in homeless accommodation, and targeted by men in the community in which they have been rehoused. Single woman and single parents are often seen as particularly 'easy targets'.

Defining male violence

There are many issues involved in defining male violence, including the question as to when an abusive act becomes a crime. One difficulty for women in getting legal protection is that the law does not reflect women's experience of violence, and charges brought often do not reflect the terror of the situation:

> On a number of occasions he has literally stood in front of me with his arms folded, stopping me from going out, and one time he even slept behind our bedroom door on the floor so I couldn't get out, I was only allowed to the toilet and back to bed, I have never told anyone that because I don't think they would believe me. I don't think it is fair the problems that face women.

> One night waiting at a bus stop to go home a man stopped beside me. It was quiet and no one about. He started talking to me 'You're beautiful' he said 'I want to shag you', and kept going on. I was scared. What could I do, ignore him? It was hard. Start running? That would be stupid. Shout for help? There was no one about. I told him to get lost, he liked that. Thankfully ... he got fed up talking because he was getting no response, told me I was an ugly bitch and went away.

This is the sort of thing that bothers me the most. There is nothing you can do, this guy walks away quite the thing, a good laugh. I can't go to the police [as] he hadn't done anything, nothing that shows anyway.

Incidents like these obviously contribute to the level of fear that women report. Although as the writer ends 'he hadn't done anything, nothing that shows anyway' - he had obviously stuck in her mind, and probably comes to mind every time she is waiting at a bus stop at night.

Many of the letters we received talked of mental cruelty and emotional abuse, yet there was a strong sense that women did not feel that this constituted a problem for which they were able to ask for help or support:

I suffered mental abuse for many years. I was made to feel stupid and worthless even though I have a good job within the civil service. If the children didn't behave perfectly, it was my fault, if they didn't get a perfect school report, it was my fault, if they got dirty when playing, it was always my fault. I could go on and on like this. I was expected to work full time and keep children and home clean and tidy, provide all meals on time, do all gardening and decorating and if I asked for help I was told I wasn't well organized. When I was too tired for sex I was told I was frigid and useless. I was left with no self-confidence. After living with just the children for three years now things are still hard but at least I have regained my self respect again and the children are much happier as there is a much better atmosphere in the house.

He started questioning everything I done and started phoning my work at every opportunity. I was getting stifled. His jealous accusations frightened me ... Soon he was hitting me and accusing me of seeing others, I couldn't convince him that I was not ... I was ashamed to tell anyone, convinced it must be my fault for making him jealous.

This woman has highlighted one of the reasons why women are less likely to ask for support in relation to emotional abuse. Suffering such abuse on a regular basis quickly erodes self-confidence and self-esteem. The following quote discusses behaviour which is hurtful and abusive but which is not illegal, a point which was reiterated in a number of other letters:

Mental cruelty, constant criticism of looks, personality, housework etc, is hard to report but potentially just as dangerous. Deprivation of your dignity by a promiscuous man who flaunts his sexual encounters is also not an offence legally, neither is the birth of two or three half

35

brothers or sisters but it is still abuse and degradation. No wages or money because it was spent on gambling, drink or other women are also abuse, these 'crimes' cannot be reported to the police.

Difficulties in naming the problem and in defining abuse are not limited to emotional abuse. Under Scottish common law the accepted definition of rape is 'the carnal knowledge of a female person by a male person obtained by overcoming her will'. For there to be 'rape' there must be penetration of the vagina by the penis, by however small an extent. This may seem very clear. However, it is not always easy for women to name their experience as rape. This is particularly the case where her will has been overcome in ways other than by physical violence or threat of physical violence.

I was forced to have sex morning and night every day for those three years even when I didn't feel good and right up until my children were born. If I didn't it was terrible, the rows, it was horrific. I could not go to sleep until he had been sexually satisfied ... Why is it he is allowed to get away with it? If he was a stranger he would be put in jail for a long time.

It was quite normal in my environment for boyfriends to try to force themselves upon a girlfriend. It seemed to be accepted as manly by both sexes. This was almost twenty years ago.

I was totally ignorant of any kind of sexual act when the man who was to become my husband gave me my first drink of alcohol. I was unconscious when he raped me. I of course became pregnant and under the rules of the time (early 50s) we got married. At the time I did not look on this as rape.

Compounding effects of male violence

Results of the survey illustrate that women are most at risk from men known to them. A number of women wrote of how previous incidents of abuse had been used against them by their partners, or of how they were afraid of asking for support for fear of being blamed or further abused.

It started I can always remember when I was about maybe 5 or 6. My brother took me to see our new house and what he did I don't think it was full sex he had with me at that time. That came later ... (You'll notice that my writing is a bit of a rush but my husband doesn't know anything about it and I don't really think he would understand. I would only get it thrown in my face every time we argued.) From

36

then on my brother used to come into our room in the morning when he just come off night-shift, and touch me and my sisters while we slept. I hated my brother and still do.

When I was a child I was touched up by one of my uncles. He did not hurt me so I did not tell anyone about it. I was only about 8 then. It was about this age when my brother started having sex with me. He told me if I told anyone he would hurt me real bad. My brother forced me to do this for about six years. I have not told anyone about this, as I have always been too frightened to discuss it ... I could not tell my husband about it either, as he could be very abusive when he wants to be.

Both these letters show the difficulties of giving an account of childhood abuse even many years later and also how pervasive control and abuse by men is. Women are blamed for the abuse they suffered as children, and sometimes the fact that they were sexually abused as a child is used as an excuse for further abuse by partners.

There are other ways in which fear of men's violence can prevent women from seeking support, for example fear that 'protective' males will react to hearing about abuse by being violent to the abuser. Women and girls may choose to suffer in silence rather than risk 'being responsible' for further violence or for 'bringing trouble' to the family. (Although women are not responsible for any revenge attacks they often feel responsible. This can be summed up by 'If I hadn't told anyone then it [the revenge] wouldn't have happened, so it is my fault').

The boy next door often asked me to masturbate him. My mum said he was only growing up and told me not to tell my dad or brothers as my dad would 'kill' him and he would get life imprisonment. The same boy next door viciously raped my six year old sister a year later.

Feeling responsible for what happens after you speak about abuse can also include feeling responsible for hurting other people's feelings. Again, women may feel forced to keep silent about abuse in order to spare other people pain:

Please note that like most women I have been able to 'manage' men until I became a widow and I have never been so disgusted with work mates, neighbours and friends - all happily married men! - who have made rude comments and suggestions (sexually). This makes it very awkward as their wife is often my friend. So because of this friendship I keep quiet and make sure I am never alone with the men. I have now been a widow for five years and speaking to other widows I find this to be a very common complaint.

Links between different forms of male violence

In considering the extent and effects of male violence, links between different forms of violence are often neglected or ignored for example, in heterosexual relationships many children witness their mother being abused by her partner and in 90 per cent of incidents the child is in the same or next room (Hughes, 1992, p.9). In the past, statutory authorities rarely considered this as reason to offer help and support to the woman and child. It was considered only necessary to intervene if a child had directly been physically injured. The woman may also have been judged as weak and inadequate because of the abuse she suffered. Recent literature suggests, however, that this situation is changing. Feminist organizations have worked along with statutory and other voluntary organizations to increase awareness about the extent and effects of domestic violence on women and children (Mullender and Morley, 1994; N.C.H., 1995). The strengths of abused women and the fact that witnessing domestic violence does have an impact on children have also been highlighted.

Research by Stark and Flitcraft (1988), highlights that there is a one in two chance of a woman being abused if her child is abused and vice versa. Studies into the effects of domestic violence on children have considered the possibility that there may also be a relationship with child sexual abuse. To examine this possibility further, the Project organized a study into links between child sexual abuse and domestic violence (Forman, 1992). Twenty women were interviewed whose children had been sexually abused by their partner. At the beginning of the study it was not known if the woman had suffered domestic violence, only that the child(ren) had been sexually abused by the woman's partner. In seventeen cases the partner was also the child's natural father.

It was discovered that every woman had suffered domestic violence to varying degrees. In only three cases was physical violence not an aspect of the abuse. Other women suffered sexual, physical and emotional violence.

The women who participated in the study were very keen to talk about their circumstances and how the sexual abuse of their children had affected their lives. This was mainly on two accounts. They wanted to pass on information that would be helpful to other women and also, many of them said that it was the first time they had the opportunity to talk about the abuse in depth, from their own point of view, without being 'judged' or 'assessed' by professionals.

Perhaps as a result of the non-judgemental nature of the interview, women began to talk about their own abuse. In order to help them name their experiences a domestic violence 'checklist' was used. This gives examples of abusive behaviour, including verbal and mental abuse. After completing the checklist fourteen women named their experiences as domestic violence for the first time. Seven women described the sexual violence as rape within marriage. In spite of the high level of violence experienced by this group, domestic violence had not been picked up as a possible occurrence, or seen as a problem during police or social work investigations of their cases of child sexual abuse.

This finding stresses the fact that domestic violence can be minimized and distorted and shows that organizations dealing with child sexual abuse do not necessarily recognize a need to give women an opportunity to talk about their own experience with the abuser. If this was done in a supportive way by someone who had an understanding of domestic violence and child sexual abuse, the woman may feel in a better position to offer help to her child. Furthermore, this approach may help mother and child understand some of the 'dynamics' of child sexual abuse. For instance, the fact that the domestic violence had been used to conceal the sexual abuse of the child makes the mother, who might be a potential source of help for the child, appear weak and powerless to thwart the abuser. Children who have witnessed their mother being put down, humiliated and physically abused are unlikely to see her as a source of support, when she has been unable to stop her own abuse. In addition, children did not want to add to their mother's pain. If their mother was going through a bad time the child did not want to make it worse, and if things were better for the mother, the child didn't want to upset her.

Women in turn thought that their children were being protected because they themselves received the brunt of abuse from their partner. Men therefore can use domestic violence to maintain the secrecy of the sexual abuse of the child and stop women from leaving the situation. One woman who took part in the research described her isolation:

> I know people don't seem to understand that, [why you do not seek help]. He was so violent that you're frightened, and I never knew there was such a thing as Women's Aid, I didn't until, just that last few months. I don't know who told me, oh no, I went down to Citizen's Advice Bureau and they put me on to it. I didn't know there was such a thing. It's funny that. When you're not out working and things like that ... you don't hear, unless you hear off somebody.

This woman's husband stopped going to work to ensure that he knew where she was at all times. When the woman finally left her husband, her child talked about being sexually abused by her father, the woman's husband. Often women are blamed for the abuse their child suffers - for not knowing or, if they knew, for not acting quickly enough. The situations that the women were in illustrate how domestic violence can distance a child from her/his mother, stopping the child going to her for help and the woman from 'seeing' the abuse. This example also emphasizes that, given the nature of abuse, children are more likely to feel safe enough to tell once they have been separated from the abuser.

Pornography can also be used to distance the child from the mother. Five women said their partners used pornography. One woman's experience of pornography illustrates how effective it can be in its portrayal of women being submissive, sexual objects, unable to help their children. She described how her husband showed the children magazines and videos when she was going out, suggesting to the children that their mother behaved in this way, and that she was going out to do this. Instead of being taught to look to adult women for support, the children were taught that women were there for exploitation by men, that women were powerless and/or complicit in fulfilling men's sexual demands.

Too often women were blamed if they did not 'see' the abuse or if they did not report their concerns. When women did report their concerns they were sometimes seen as being vindictive. One woman, who was not believed by professionals, had to send her children on access visits:

> I kept saying [my daughter] doesn't want to go ... [they said] you have to make her ... she's getting bad vibes from you ... don't ask her any questions when she comes back from her access visits, because it would go against you in court. I was terrified to ask my child anything and that's the point - I should have been asking her because she was abused in access, my two children were abused in access and we have proof of that, and they were badly abused from what we found out.

In this case the lack of recognition of links between different forms of abuse by helping agencies actually facilitated the child abuse. Highlighting the links between different forms of violence is important as it raises awareness about the extent of male violence and helps women deal with the compounded effects of past and present abuse. For example, feelings of self-blame, isolation and helplessness may be exacerbated if a woman has lived with more than one abusive man, if she has had more than one abusive experience, or if her children have also been abused.

Women's and children's position in society has to be viewed as a whole. Women are seen as mothers, wives, daughters and carers, putting others' needs before their own. They are expected to be responsible for the protection of their children and the control of their partners. One woman described the dilemma of being caught between two socially prescribed roles:

I was trying to support my daughter, be there for my husband, just in case this was a big mistake, I felt I just couldn't turn my back on him, what if he hadn't done this. Although I was staying away from him I felt I've got to be there to show support for both. You feel as if you've got to be the tower of strength for everyone.

This example shows a woman putting her own feelings into second place. This is often the case for abused women. Women abused as children are afraid to ask for support for fear it will trigger violence from partners; women and girls who suffer rape may be fearful of a violent response from husbands, brothers or fathers; women whose children have been sexually abused by their partner are expected to respond as mothers first and little space, if any, is offered for their own needs and feelings. All these examples have a common element in that the abused woman or child, although they have not caused the abuse, is forced to carry responsibility for the consequences of that abuse.

Changing the focus - putting responsibility with the abusers

Two main aims of the work of the Women's Support Project have been to increase understanding of male violence by analysing the links between different forms of such violence; and to name individual acts of violence as male abuse of power in the context of a patriarchal society. This message has recently been reinforced by the development of a Scottish campaign of 'Zero Tolerance' of male violence. The campaign was initially developed by Edinburgh District Council Women's Committee and has since been adopted by a number of local authorities across Britain.

The Zero Tolerance campaign aims to put across the public education message that male violence against women and children is wrong; that it is a crime; and that there can be no excuses nor justifications for the use of violence.

The initial stages of the campaign, which was first launched in Edinburgh in 1993, involved public advertising and a series of events focusing on different aspects of violence. The posters, which are printed in stark black and white, portray strong positive images of women which contrast sharply with the text. The poster on domestic violence, for example, uses the image of a woman relaxing in her own sitting room obviously in a fairly well off household. The text reports 'She lives with a successful businessman, loving father and respected member of the community. Last week he hospitalized her'. (See chapter 3). Other posters focus on child sexual abuse and rape. All posters are linked by the use of the slogan 'Male abuse of power is a crime', and by

41

the striking black and white images used in all materials. The final poster in the first stage of the campaign simply said 'No man has the right'.

This is the first time in this country that male violence has been actively and publicly condemned by those who provide services such as health care, education, housing, social work, and police. It is the first time that such a large scale campaign has said 'Male violence is wrong - and there are no excuses'.

The images used in the Zero Tolerance campaign make it much harder to continue hiding behind the myths around male violence. The images show ordinary women in nice homes. The whole point is that it could be any woman, abused by any man. The Campaign has been attacked from a number of quarters as being 'anti-men'. The message of Zero Tolerance is not anti-men. It is anti-male violence.

Public education campaigns such as Zero Tolerance require resources and there have been objections to using public funds in this way. In considering the costs we have to remember that we all already pay for male violence in a variety of ways, for instance in housing, police, courts and prison, social security, legal aid, hospital and medical care, child care and criminal injuries compensation. In addition to these public costs the individual abused woman pays dearly, in the financial sense, and in other ways which are harder to measure. How can we judge what a woman could have achieved, how much more she might have been able to offer to her community if she had been able to live without the fear of violence?

Bibliography

Bell, P. and Macleod, J. (1989), 'Survey on extent of violence against women' (unpublished report), The Women's Support Project, Glasgow.

C.O.S.L.A. (1991), *Women and Violence: Report of Working Party*, Convention of Scottish Local Authorities, Edinburgh.

Forman, J. (1992), 'Is there a correlation between child sexual abuse and domestic violence? - An exploratory study of the links between child sexual abuse and domestic violence in a sample of intrafamilial child sexual abuse cases', (unpublished report), The Women's Support Project, Glasgow.

Hughes, H. (1992), 'Impact of spouse abuse on children of battered women', *Violence Update*, pp. 9-11.

Kelly, L. (1989), *Surviving Sexual Violence*, Polity Press, Cambridge.

Mullender, A. and Morley, R. (1994), *Children Living with Domestic Violence*, Whiting and Birch, London.

NCH Action for Children. (1995), *The Hidden Victims - Children and Domestic Violence*, NCH Action for Children, London.

Saunders, A., Epstein, C., Keep, G. and Debbonaire, T. (1995), *It hurts me too - Children's Experiences of Domestic Violence and Refuge Life*, Women's Aid Federation of England, Bristol.

Scottish Women's Aid (1993), Scottish Women's Aid Annual Report, Edinburgh.

Scottish Women's Aid (1989), *Women Talking To Women: A Women's Aid Approach to Counselling*, Edinburgh.

Stark, E. and Flitcraft, A.H. (1988), 'Women and children at risk - a feminist perspective on child abuse', *International Journal of Health Services*, Vol. 18, No. 1, pp. 97-118.

Strathclyde Rape Crisis (1993), Strathclyde Rape Crisis Centre Annual Report, Glasgow.

3 Public place, private issue? The public's reaction to the Zero Tolerance campaign against violence against women

Kate Hunt and Jenny Kitzinger

Introduction: the social and political background to the Zero Tolerance campaign

> In the last five or six years, domestic violence has been in the public eye as it never has before. Various governments now tell us that violence in the home is a crime and that it is not to be tolerated. Statutory and voluntary agencies say that it is unacceptable. International proclamations are made... After years of campaigning, domestic violence is firmly on the public agenda. Finally we can talk about it. It is no longer a secret. (Hague and Malos, 1993, pp. 2-3).

But why should domestic violence ever have been secret, and what are the consequences of this secrecy? What has changed, and how far-reaching are these changes? This chapter explores how ideas about 'privacy' and 'the family' have been used to protect men who assault women and children. It goes on to examine the nature of, and public reactions to, a particular campaign, 'the Zero Tolerance campaign', which sought to challenge and re-define such violence.

Historically, there has been little protection for women against physical and sexual assault. What legal safeguard did exist emanated from laws designed to protect men's property. A man (if not a serf or slave) was protected from another man's theft or abuse of his animals, his servants and members of his family, but his wife and children received no protection under the law if he chose to abuse them. Until recently in England a man could not be convicted of raping his wife and many laws which might protect against physical or sexual assault from a stranger have not been applied to assault from one's husband (Schwendinger and Schwendinger, 1983). Male violence against women was not so much secret as an unnamed 'fact of life' for women or a 'right' for men. Indeed, a certain amount of violence was judicially legitimated. The common expression 'a rule of thumb' comes from the 1782 declaration by Judge Buler that legally a husband could beat his wife as long as he did not use a stick thicker than his thumb (Pahl, 1985, p. 11). The idea that violence is an appropriate strategy to control a 'nagging' wife or punish an unfaithful one has continued to be implicit, and sometimes explicit, in many court rulings since then. For example, in 1975 a Scottish sheriff expressed his support for the ancient principle that 'reasonable chastisement should be the duty of every husband if his wife misbehaves' (Freeman, 1992, p. 126) and a woman's 'provocative' behaviour is still routinely cited in defence of the husbands and boyfriends who murder them (Radford and Russell, 1992).

The legal and social legitimation of physical and sexual violence against women within the home has prevented 'domestic violence' from being seen as a public problem. Indeed, such violence was often entirely unacknowledged. In 1971 the North American sociologist Diana Russell applied to the National Science Foundation for funding for her study of rape in marriage. She received a letter in response telling her 'You have not made it clear that rape is an important problem or whether it is just the concern of a bunch of loony women' (Russell, 1990). Even now, when so many women and children have spoken out about abuse within the home, such abuses are sometimes perceived as a minority concern and the media persist in presenting the home as a sanctuary and the streets as the main sites of danger for women (Soothill and Walby, 1991; Kitzinger and Skidmore, 1995) [1].

The failure to address violence within the home has been inextricably intertwined with notions of 'privacy' and the idea that 'an Englishman's home is his castle'. Brutality against women has been shrouded by the sanctity of marriage, friends and relatives hesitating to get involved in 'family' affairs and to 'come between man and wife'. Victimization was identified as women's individual responsibility, 'You've made your bed , you must lie on it' (Hall et al., 1981). As one woman commented about the reaction of her family and friends: 'they knew I was getting beat up but they put it this way - that it was our lives and that we had to sort it out for ourselves' (quoted in Homer et al., 1985, p. 105).

At the same time the state's responses to violence against women via the police, social work, or medical profession have been muted (Hoff, 1990). As one study concluded: 'There is a marked reluctance on the part of all practitioners to become involved in cases of marital violence which they see as peripheral to their main concerns. The privacy of the family and of marriage is constantly stressed.' (Johnson, 1985, p. 109). Beating one's wife has not been treated as a criminal offence and, until recently, a common police response was to remain as uninvolved as possible (Pahl, 1985, p. 17). Such tactics, as Edwards has remarked, 'reflects the relegation of private or domestic 'crime' to that of lowest priority' (Edwards, 1989, p. 5).

The consequences of the privacy surrounding much violence against women are that there are pitiful gaps in our knowledge about these forms of violence and woefully inadequate services, partly because of the serious underestimation of the extent of the problem (Mooney, 1994). Men have not been challenged for their actions and women were left feeling isolated and personally responsible for the violence perpetrated against them. The silence surrounding childhood sexual abuse has increased children's vulnerability and shame. The failure publicly to condemn rape in marriage made it hard for wives to name and resist such assaults. As long as society insists that 'domestic violence' is a purely personal problem then, as Hoff points out, women will be forced to seek 'personal solutions':

> Thus a woman may be beaten again and again not because she likes it, has learned to be helpless, or fails to follow through when pressing charges, etc. Rather she is acting in a pattern that logically follows from a definition of battering as primarily an interpersonal private matter between intimates (Hoff 1990, p. 78).

However, over the past two centuries there has been an ongoing struggle to challenge male violence and to redefine rape, sexual assault, and all other forms of 'domestic violence' as a public problem. The history of oppressive legal rulings has been paralleled by a history of resistance, not only from individual victimized women but also from collectivities of women and sometimes the community as a whole. In nineteenth century England, for example, villagers would march towards the cottage of a man known to beat his wife blowing cows' horns and drumming kettles and chanting: 'There is a man in this place/ Has beat his wife/ Has beat his wife/ It is a very great shame and disgrace/ To all who live in this place'. In this way the entire community marked its disapproval of such abuse (Horley, 1990). Individually and collectively there have also been concerted efforts to reform the law and make provisions for women and children assaulted in their homes. In 1829 in Britain, the law allowing the chastisement of wives was repealed. In the

1870s Frances Power Cobbe's paper, 'Wife Torture in England', and the resulting outcry helped to bring about the Matrimonial Causes Act, giving women the right to a legal separation and maintenance if their husband had been convicted of aggravated assault. Almost a century later Erin Pizzey's book, 'Scream Quietly or the Neighbours will hear', and the emerging feminist network of refuges for women, influenced the setting up of the 1974 Parliamentary Select committee on Violence in Marriage (Pizzey, 1974). More recently feminist campaigns and the personal testimony of survivors have led to the increasing criminalization of rape within marriage and the recognition of widespread sexual assaults against children (Hall, 1981; Borokowski et al., 1983).

The Zero Tolerance campaign launched in 1992 built on, and contributed to, this history of challenges to male violence. It was explicitly designed to confront the continuing invisibility and legitimization of violence against women. It aimed to promote the profile of the issue on the national agenda and to transform private shame into public outrage. The rest of this chapter describes this campaign and examines public responses to this very overt challenge to violence against women.

Re-defining violence: the nature of the Zero Tolerance campaign

The campaign was conducted by the Women's Committee at Edinburgh District Council with advice from groups directly involved in combating violence against women and with design work and photography by the feminist photographer Franki Raffles [2]. The campaign was launched partly in response to Edinburgh District Council's own research which found that fear of violence was one of the top three issues of concern to women in Edinburgh (Stevenson, 1993). The campaign was also influenced by other research, conducted in Edinburgh schools, which found a high acceptance of violence among young people and greater tolerance of a man beating his wife than his girlfriend (Falchacar, 1992).

The initial phase of the campaign consisted of a series of four posters that were displayed on billboards, bus stops and in other public places throughout Edinburgh. The campaign also involved the display of giant placards bearing statements about male violence which ran the length of Princes Street (Edinburgh's main shopping street and an important centre for its tourist industry). The placards bore simple white-on-black statements about the nature and frequency of violence against women. In addition, leaflets and other material were widely distributed and one local daily newspaper, the *Evening News*, ran a series of feature and news articles which were openly supportive of the campaign (Kitzinger and Hunt, 1994).

The Zero Tolerance campaign sought to raise public awareness of the extent and nature of male violence, and to tackle many of the misconceptions consequent on the legacy of secrecy and taboo around this issue. It provided three main challenges to some of the problems surrounding violence against women discussed above.

Firstly, it made uncompromising statements about the unacceptability of abuse and the necessity to bring violence against women under the public criminal justice system. Instead of advising individual women how to protect themselves it explicitly challenged the social sanctioning of male violence and clearly located the responsibility with society as a whole, and men in particular. Two of the main placards simply bore the statements: 'No Man has the Right' and 'Male Abuse of Power is a Crime' (and the latter statement appeared on the bottom of every poster).

Secondly, the campaign drew attention to the fact that most violence against women is from men whom they know and that it occurs in all classes of society. Statements on the placards included: 'Almost 50% of women murdered are killed by a partner or ex-partner' and '85% of rapists are men known to the victim'. The posters reinforced this message. They portrayed cosy, affluent, domestic scenes tastefully shot in black and white: a woman reading in front of the fire; two children playing with a doll's house; and a young child and her (presumed) grandmother reading a book together. The images all suggested 'safety', 'warmth' and 'security', but were undercut with captions suggesting the hidden abuse that lay behind the scenes of apparent comfort: 'She lives with a successful business man, loving father and respected member of the community. Last week he hospitalised her'; 'By the time they reach eighteen, one of them will have been subjected to sexual abuse'; 'From three to ninety three, women are raped'. Where the media gives disproportionate attention to attacks by strangers, the Zero Tolerance campaign thus named fathers, brothers and friends as possible assailants. Where media images repeatedly represent dark alleyways or deserted wasteland as primary sites of danger, the Zero Tolerance posters showed domestic interiors, highlighting the violence that goes on behind closed doors. Thus the campaign dealt subtly, but powerfully, with the false antithesis between public and private which is endemic to much of the presentation of violence against women (so evident even in the terminology, such as 'domestic' violence).

Thirdly, the design and siting of the campaign material clearly located the issue of violence against women in the public domain. In group discussions with members of the public it was clear that the very glossy quality of the posters and the prestigious situation of the placards challenged the 'sordid' nature of the subject. The fact that the campaign was funded by local government also gave it status and the stamp of respectability. Above all, the very size and boldness of the campaign's presentation helped to refute the idea that such violence should be hidden away as a private shame. As one survivor of childhood sexual abuse, describing her reaction, explained:

> When all the posters were up along the tripods right along Princes Street ... I couldn't believe it. I was going along in the bus and I thought: 'There's one there. There's another one! They haven't got them all along Princes Street ... YES! They have! It was very good. [I felt] Yes, this is what I want. I want people to see this. (Incest survivors' self-help group).

This woman was clearly positive about the campaign, but how representative are such reactions? In order to explore the response of the general public to such material we conducted a street survey. The following section of this chapter details the findings of this study and also draws on focus group discussions with different professional groups, other interest groups (such as the incest survivors' self-help group), and members of the general public.

Assessing public reactions: the street survey

The survey was conducted as part of a broader evaluation of the first six months of Edinburgh's Zero Tolerance campaign, and it was designed to complement detailed focus group discussions. In addressing the public's reaction to the campaign we focus here mainly on the street survey, although some reference is made to material from the group discussions.

The street survey was undertaken in late May 1993 in Princes Street. A total of 228 interviews were conducted resulting in a sample which reflected the age, sex and class composition of Edinburgh (apart from slightly over-representing people under 30). The majority of the respondents (83 per cent) were resident in Edinburgh. Most of the remainder (11 per cent) lived within 50 miles of the city. Most people (80 per cent) had travelled through Princes Street regularly in the last month (at least once a week). The majority of respondents had, therefore, had ample opportunity to observe the campaign's placards, and the survey largely canvassed the opinion of a local resident (rather than tourist) population.

Before being asked about the campaign itself, the sample were asked to express their agreement or otherwise with a number of questions which ascertained how traditional their views were on gender roles, whether they felt that violence against women should be criminalized, and aspects of their knowledge about violence against women. Most of the sample did not hold very traditional views about gender roles. For example, the majority (75 per cent) disagreed with the statement that 'Some equality in marriage is a good thing, but by and large the husband should have the main say-so in family matters'. Most seemed to agree with the campaign emphasis on violence against women as a crime. Over 90 per cent of the sample agreed with the statement that 'Men who abuse are criminals and should be treated as such'. The three questions on knowledge about violence elicited more ambivalent responses: 18 per cent neither agreed nor disagreed with the statement 'Battered women come from all walks of life. Social class, family and racial background make no difference'; 22 per cent neither agreed nor disagreed that 'If domestic violence happens once it is more likely to happen again'; and 44 per cent neither agreed nor disagreed that 'Nearly half of the attacks on women take place in front of observers'.

Public reaction to the Zero Tolerance campaign

Did the campaign succeed in attracting attention? One of the main long term aims of the Edinburgh Zero Tolerance campaign was to generate wider debate about violence against women and children. The street survey provides evidence that the campaign successfully attracted attention to the issue. Sixty four percent of those interviewed already knew about the campaign before coming to Princes Street on the day of the interview. Perhaps more importantly, 39 per cent of those who already knew about the campaign had not only seen it, or heard about it, but had actually discussed the campaign with someone else. As one police officer in a focus group discussion commented: 'They [the advertisements] were controversial, they got people talking about it'.

How was the campaign received by the public? Public responses to the Zero Tolerance campaign were generally positive. Interviewees who already knew about the campaign were asked to describe their feelings about it: 79 per cent said they felt positive, while just 6 per cent described their feelings as negative. The positive feelings were explained in the group discussions with comments ranging from: 'It's good, it's making you think' (Transport workers, male), to 'It's like some injection of power, that brings you courage, and you just feel great' (Shakti women's group, female).

In order to elicit some reactions to the campaign from the whole survey sample, everyone was asked how much they agreed or disagreed with two statements: 'Edinburgh is right to take the lead in drawing attention to domestic violence and abuse' and 'The display of posters in Princes Street as part of the Zero Tolerance campaign is bad for Edinburgh's image'. Only 4 per cent disagreed with the statement that the city was 'right to take the lead in drawing attention to domestic violence and abuse', while only 11 per cent agreed that the Zero Tolerance campaign was bad for Edinburgh's image.

In the group discussions those who were critical of the public display of the campaign material made comments such as: 'Princes Street is for tourists. They [the posters] shouldn't be there at all' (Office workers), and 'It wasn't suitable for Princes Street. That's not what these big stands are for, they are there to beautify the city' (Christian women's guild group). By contrast, those supportive of drawing attention to violence against women in this way applauded the high-profile nature of the campaign: '[People should be] proud that the city's taking on something like this and put it in the most noticeable place in Edinburgh' (Women's Aid workers).

One concern was that the Zero Tolerance posters could confront people with their own experiences of violence in a very traumatic way - 'rubbing their nose in it'. Certainly one complaint to the District Council came from a woman in her sixties who said she preferred to forget what had happened to her and did not want to be reminded. However, most of the respondents to the questionnaire survey, and participants in the group discussions, did not seem to feel this way. Instead, many research participants who had been assaulted said they welcomed the posters. Being confronted with the unpleasant facts was seen as necessary and far preferable to ignoring the problem. 'It's the **silence** that's rubbing our nose in it, that kind of common notion of 'keep it quiet'. That's shoving your nose down all the time' (Incest survivors' self-help group).

To look in more detail at the public's reaction to the campaign, data from the two street survey statements about the city's role in the campaign were combined. The combined responses identify those who were most positive and most negative about the campaign and enable us to check that people who held apparently contradictory views on these questions were relatively few in number. Sixty two per cent of respondents were labelled as 'wholly positive'; these were the people who thought that Edinburgh was right to 'take the lead in drawing attention to domestic violence and abuse' and rejected the notion that the display of the Zero Tolerance posters in Princes Street was bad for Edinburgh's image. Just 12 per cent were classified as having 'any negative' feelings about the campaign; these were people who did not think that Edinburgh was right to take the lead and/or thought that the display of posters in Princes Street was bad for Edinburgh's image. Just 6 people expressed negative views on both statements, and a further 10 people were negative about one statement and neutral about the other. Only 10 people had apparently contradictory views, expressing support for the campaign in response to one question but not the other. The remainder of the interviewees (26 per cent) were classified as having expressed 'some equivocal feelings'. This comprised of 20 interviewees who were neutral (neither agreed nor disagreed) about both statements, and 35 interviewees who expressed positive support for the campaign in one statement, but were neutral about the other.

Using this combined score to classify people's responses to the campaign it was clear that those with positive feelings about the campaign were more likely to agree with statistics about violence used elsewhere in the Zero Tolerance campaign (Kitzinger and Hunt, 1994). Presumably this reflects both the predisposition of those who are better informed about male violence to endorse the campaign, and that the campaign has been successful in raising public awareness about violence.

The public's perception of the need for a public campaign around violence. The final part of the street survey directly questioned the acceptability of, and the perceived need for, public discussion and information around violence against women. Two statements were presented. Less than 10 per cent of interviewees thought that 'Violence against women is not the sort of issue that should be publicly discussed': while nearly three quarters of the sample agreed that 'The public as a whole do not know enough about violence and abuse'. This is strong evidence for the acceptance of open discussion of violence against women, and suggests further support for the campaign in raising the profile of violence against women as an important issue for public debate. As one woman commented in a group discussion: 'The council definitely deserve a round of applause for that, because they're relieving the burden of bringing [the subject of sexual abuse] up into everyday life from the people who are affected by it' (Incest survivors' self-help group).

Responses to both statements about the public discussion of, and knowledge about, violence were examined in relation to people's feelings about the campaign. Among interviewees who were 'wholly positive' about the campaign almost all (97 per cent) disagreed with the statement that 'Violence against women is not the sort of issue that should be publicly discussed', compared with only 22 per cent of those who had expressed any negative reaction to the campaign. The contrast between those who were most positive and those most negative about the campaign also showed in responses to the question about public ignorance about domestic violence and abuse. Nearly all (93 per cent) of the positive group thought that the public were not sufficiently well informed about violence and abuse, as compared with just 39 per cent of the most negative.

The combined evidence from these questions strongly suggests that the public is ready for, and predominantly accepting of, the Zero Tolerance campaign. However, discussion of these data would not be complete without some reference to differences within the sample by age, housing tenure (our proxy for class) and gender (see Kitzinger and Hunt, 1994 for more details). Younger respondents tended to be in greater agreement with the campaign than their older counterparts. They were more likely to know about the Zero Tolerance campaign and to have discussed it with friends, relatives or colleagues. They were also more likely to feel that the campaign did not damage Edinburgh's image and that it was acceptable to discuss violence against women in public. They were less likely to hold traditional views of sex roles and were more likely to strongly agree that abusers should be treated as criminals.

Similar patterns are evident when comparing male and female respondents. Women were more likely than men to be very positive about the campaign and to have discussed the Zero Tolerance material. They were also more likely to strongly agree that Edinburgh had been right to adopt the campaign and to disagree with the statement that the campaign might damage the city's public image. They were more likely strongly to reject the suggestion that violence against women should not be publicly discussed and to strongly agree that the public are ignorant on this matter. More women than men strongly rejected traditional sex roles, and more strongly agreed that 'Men who abuse are criminals and should be treated as such'.

Differences by housing tenure (our proxy for class) were fewer and far less marked. However, people living in owner-occupied accommodation were more likely to be wholly positive about the campaign (69 per cent vs. 53 per cent) and less likely to express any negative feelings (20 per cent vs. 35 per cent) than people in other tenure groups.

Overall then, the public were supportive of the campaign and this was true of the majority of people even within the least supportive demographic groups. The risks the campaign took in publicly challenging 'private' violence have not alienated the majority of people, and the particularly strong support for the campaign among the younger population may suggest that it was an idea whose time had come.

Conclusion

Much violence against women has a long history of being viewed as 'private', beyond public gaze, comment or debate. Such violence is sanctioned within the privacy of the home, and often within the 'privacy' of a sexual relationship between a man and his female partner. Whilst notions of privacy often surround both the family and sex, British society demonstrates a great deal of ambivalence about public discussions of both. On the one hand, it is often argued that the publicizing of the 'private' lives of the rich and infamous is in the 'public interest' (as evidenced by recent coverage of the affairs of Tory ministers and Royal family members) whilst, on the other, the 'public' are often used as a rhetorical device either to limit discussion of sensitive areas, or to justify exposure of others.

However, when the value of privacy is promoted, it is necessary to ask 'whose privacy?'. Traditionally, the privacy with which the family has been enshrined has meant the 'privacy' of some men to abuse. Female privacy is less sacrosanct and being black, unemployed, working class, foreign or not heterosexual increases people's exposure to intrusions by the state into their 'personal lives'. The Child Support Agency can punish the mother who fails to disclose the identity of her child's father; anyone receiving state benefits can be interrogated about cohabitation arrangements; cross-questioning lesbians about their sex lives is seen as pertinent to their fitness as parents; immigration regulations allow for the systematic invasions of privacy by the state. Thus, there is a double standard surrounding the notion of 'privacy'. Privacy has always been a resource more carefully guarded on behalf of the middle class, heterosexual, white male. Far from protecting women, in many circumstances the ideology of privacy has been used selectively as an oppressive tool. As Pahl points out, an emphasis on 'protecting privacy' can work to the detriment of those who are weaker within the social and physical space defined as private (Dahl and Snare, 1978; Pahl, 1985, p.19).

But the power of the ideology of 'privacy' to protect men who abuse women and children has begun to wane. The public seem to be willing to confront many more so-called private problems than one might think. It seems that the caution in disseminating information or generating public debate has often been ill-placed, proving to reflect more about the sensitivities of the speaker than the people whom they claim to represent. It is often assumed for example, that public discussion of sex is impossible. The Government themselves supported this attitude when they intervened in the funding process of a large national survey of sex which sought to gather crucial information which would aid the prevention of the spread of HIV (See 'Thatcher halts survey on sex', *The Sunday Times*, 10 September 1989 and Johnson et al., 1994, p. vii). However, as the Chief Medical Officer pointed out:

> The high response rate [to the National Survey of Sex] shows beyond a peradventure that most members of the public will accept and co-operate with the efforts of responsible people working to protect and improve their health in the sensitive area of sex. This was also the experience of my predecessor ... who during World War II first used the mass media ... to give advice on 'venereal disease' ... Neither of

us received complaints or criticisms for discussing frankly in public, subjects previously regarded as taboo.

The Zero Tolerance campaign sought to confront attitudes towards another supposedly taboo subject, and to do so in strong and unambiguous terms. Our survey results suggest that the public have been far more accepting of this campaign then many might have predicted beforehand. There seems to be positive enthusiasm and support for efforts to challenge violence against women and, in this sense, the Zero Tolerance campaign can clearly claim success. The campaign has already been adopted in other parts of Britain and has also attracted much attention internationally. It was cited in a recent Parliamentary debate (House of Commons, 1993) about domestic violence (which followed the publication of the Third Report from the Home Affairs Committee of Session 1992-3 on Domestic Violence) which demonstrated strong cross-party support for the need for action on the 'devastating problem of domestic violence'. It seems that attitudes are beginning to change and that the Zero Tolerance campaign has had an important role to play in that transformation.

However, those who have been active in the struggle against domestic violence for many years might be forgiven for asking how extensive this change is. It is all very well putting up bold advertisements apparently with wide public support, but violence against women remains an extremely serious, and largely untouched, problem. Several members of parliament expressed their concern about the lack of Government action; raising awareness is an important and necessary step, but ineffective without the resources to follow it up. Where the Department of Health is 'funding the Women's Aid Federation to the tune of £136,000' the Canadian government are spending $136 million to combat domestic violence (House of Commons, 1993, p.382). The Zero Tolerance campaign has helped to assert the importance of the issue. However, as Hague and Malos have commented, 'We have yet to see whether the public attention will last, and whether the political will is there to implement the changes needed in comprehensive ways' (Hague and Malos, 1993, p.2).

Postscript

The campaign has met with its detractors. Under the headline 'Zero Tolerance doesn't add up' the Sunday Times (23/10/94) reported that some people branded the campaign 'ultra-feminist' and 'anti-male' and challenged the validity of the statistics that it displayed. The report included criticism from the Lord Provost of Edinburgh and from Malcolm Rifkind MP. Under the headline: 'Time to give Zero Tolerance to the sex warriors' Gerald

Warner (Sunday Times, 9/10/94) went further and condemned the campaign as 'poisonous', 'a grotesque libel' and a 'Goebbels-style exercise in hate propaganda'. A further evaluation of the campaign when it was adopted in Strathclyde revealed resistance to the campaign from some professional groups (e.g. the police) and certainly suggests that the potential for a backlash exists.

Notes

1. It took some time for the second wave of feminism to 're-discover' the fact that danger could be inside the home as well as outside on the streets. A book written from an explicitly feminist framework, published in 1974, contained a chapter on 'Dangerous Places' in which the only subheadings were 'on the streets' and 'in your car'. Another chapter on 'How to avoid rape' was subdivided into three sections: 'locks', 'securing your home or apartment' and 'answering the door and telephone'. Protecting oneself from the men one lives with is not discussed (Horos, 1974).
2. Franki Raffles died in December 1994 after giving birth to twin daughters. She will be sadly missed by all those who knew her personally and professionally. We would like to dedicate this chapter to her memory.

Bibliography

Borokowski, M., Murch, M. and Walker, V. (1983), *Marital Violence: the Community Response*, Tavistock Publications, London.

Dahl, T. and Snare, A. (1978), 'The coercion of privacy: a feminist perspective' in Smart, C. and Smart, B. (eds.), *Women, Sexuality and Social Control*, Routledge and Kegan Paul, London, pp. 9-26.

Edwards, S.S.M. (1989), *Policing 'Domestic' Violence. Women, the Law and the State*, Reprinted 1991 edition, Sage Publications Ltd, London.

Falchacar, N. (1992), *Adolescents' Knowledge about, and Attitudes to, Domestic Violence*, Edinburgh District Council Women's Committee, Edinburgh.

Freeman, M. (1992), 'Doing his best to sustain the sanctity of marriage' in Johnson, N. (ed.), *Marital Violence*, Routledge and Kegan Paul, London, pp. 124-46.

Hague, G. and Malos, E. (1993), *Domestic Violence. Action for Change*, New Clarion Press, Cheltenham.

Hall, R., Jame, S. and Kertesz, J. (1981), *The Rapist who Pays the Rent*, Falling Wall Press, Bristol.

Hoff, L.A. (1990), *Battered Women as Survivors*, Routledge, London.

Homer, S., Leonard, A. and Taylor, P. (1985), 'Personal relationships: help and hindrance' in Johnson, N. (ed.), *Marital Violence*, Routledge and Kegan Paul, London, pp. 93-108.

Horley, S. (1990), 'A shame and a disgrace', *Social Work Today*, Vol. 21, No. 41, pp. 16-7.

Horos, C. (1974), *Rape*, Tobey Publishing, New Canaan.

House of Commons (1993), Proceedings of Parliamentary Debate on Domestic Violence, 21 July 1993.

Johnson, A., Wadsworth, J., Wellings, K., Field, J. and Bradshaw, S. (1994), *Sexual Attitudes and Lifestyles*, Blackwell Scientific Publications, Oxford.

Johnson, N. (1985), 'Police, social work and medical responses to battered women' in Johnson, N. (ed.), *Marital Violence*, Routledge and Kegan Paul, London, pp. 109-23.

Kitzinger, J. and Hunt, K. (1994), *Evaluation of Edinburgh District Council's Zero Tolerance Campaign. Full Report*, Edinburgh District Council Women's Committee, Edinburgh.

Kitzinger, J. and Skidmore, P. (1995), 'Playing safe: media coverage of the prevention of child sexual abuse', *Child Abuse Review*, Vol. 4, pp. 47-56.

Mooney, J. (1994), *The hidden figure: domestic violence in North London. Findings of a survey conducted on domestic violence in the north London Borough of Islington*, Centre for Criminology, Middlesex University and Islington Council, produced by Islington's Police and Crime Prevention Unit.

Pahl, J. (ed.), (1985), *Private Violence and Public Policy: The Needs of Battered Women and the Response of Public Services*, Routledge and Kegan Paul, London.

Pizzey, E. (1974), *Scream Quietly or the Neighbours will Hear*, Penguin, Middlesex.

Radford, J. and Russell, D. (eds.). (1992), *Femicide: the Politics of Woman Killing*, Open University Press, Milton Keynes.

Russell, D. (1990), *Rape in Marriage*, Indiana University Press, Indianapolis.

Schwendinger, J. and Schwendinger, H. (1983), *Rape and Inequality*, Sage, London.

Soothill, K. and Walby, S. (1991), *Sex Crime in the News*, Routledge, London.

Stevenson, B. (1993), Women's Consultation Exercise, Edinburgh District Council Women's Committee.

4 Violence and vulnerability: Conditions of work for streetworking prostitutes

Marina A. Barnard

Introduction

The health risks associated with prostitution have very often been considered in terms of the potential spread of sexually transmitted infections. In the most recent past this concern has focused on the possibility that prostitution will act as a bridgehead for HIV infection to spread in the general population. The tendency has been to look at the health risks prostitutes pose to others rather than the risks accruing to prostitutes in consequence of the work they do. Possibly the occupational health risks of prostitution have escaped attention because selling sex is not generally considered a legitimate vocation. Nonetheless, there are significant occupational hazards associated with prostitution (Faugier et al., 1992; McLeod, 1982). Perhaps the most important of these relate to the potential for client violence. It is apparent from a number of reports on prostitution that the risks of client violence are an integral part of selling sexual services (Synn-Stern, 1992; French, 1990; Silbert, 1981). Prostitutes in this research, and in others, variously reported a range of attacks by clients from being abducted to being punched and raped. In the course of this study one prostitute was murdered. Defining the health risks of prostitution solely in terms of the potential public health risks of sexually transmitted infection takes too narrow a view of the dangers associated with prostitution. Concentrating on the ways in which prostitutes represent a threat to the health of others suggests that the health needs of prostitutes themselves are, at best, unrecognized and at worst, considered unimportant.

This paper will look at the dynamics of the commercial sexual encounter in terms of the exercise of power between prostitutes and their clients and the potential for violence to erupt. The ways in which prostitutes try to establish client compliance is a particular focus. Securing control of the commercial sex encounter was often articulated by the women in this study as a critical factor in their work. This was not only from the point of view of ensuring proper payment but also in terms of personal safety. There were a number of ways in which the women sought to manage their dealings with clients so as to minimize the likelihood of trouble erupting. However, these strategies were not always successful. Some clients did not accept the women's conditions of business and would use physical intimidation to force them to accede to their demands, sexual or otherwise. Situations where client compliance could not be secured because of intimidation on the part of the client are reported upon. The social structural determinants of violence directed at women in the context of streetworking prostitution are examined. In addition, I will discuss the ways in which women respond to these situations given that they are illegally involved in a heavily stigmatized profession. This paper will end with a consideration of possible policy initiatives to curtail the potential for violence directed at women who prostitute.

However, to start with it is worthwhile pointing out that the potential for violence is not unique to the commercial sexual encounter. If, as many researchers would argue, there are links between gender and power and its manifestation in violence, then violence in the context of commercial sexual encounters may well have features in common with other kinds of violence against women. It is therefore valuable to begin by considering violence in other settings; in the broader context of normative gender role expectations and the influence that these exert on male/female relations.

Violence against women and prostitution

Sexual violence and violence within families have in common the fact that the victims are overwhelmingly female (Russell, 1984; Dobash et al., 1992). Research on violence against women points to social structural inequities in the distribution of power, authority, and control between men and women (Hamner and Maynard, 1987; Green et al., 1987). Scully (1990), in a study of convicted rapists, argues that it is the structural subordination of women which lies at the heart of violence against women whether it is sexual violence or within the family. In this sense violence, she asserts, is a symptom, not the cause, of the larger social problem. Normative expectations of male dominance structurally realized in the workings of society and manifest in relations between men and women form the larger social problem. As Clark and Lewis comment, 'the maintenance of this position of authority must to a greater or lesser extent rely upon the threat or reality of violence'

(1977, p.176). Dobash and Dobash (1979), in a study of domestic violence, argue that the motivation for attacks often centres around the notion of 'keeping a woman in her place'. Male role socialization incorporates the notion that women are subordinate, that men should have control over women, and that men should protect as well as have the right to punish and discipline women (Scully, 1990; Sanday, 1986; Dobash and Dobash, 1979; Evason,1982). Scully's study of rapists provides evidence that some men used rape as a means of asserting their dominance over women. Rape was also used by some men as revenge and punishment (1990). Relatedly, Chesler (1978) found in interviews with men that a desire to dominate was an enduring male fantasy.

A related theme running through accounts of violence against women concerns the rigidity with which women's roles are normatively defined and the importance attaching to sexual reputation. A good woman is ideally a wife and a mother whose sexuality is only expressed within the confines of her relationship with her partner (Horowitz, 1981; Dobash and Dobash, 1979). From a very early age girls are made aware of the link between social respectability and sexual purity (James, 1986; Holland et al., 1992). A woman who is seen to be sexually available risks losing her reputation. This is not the case for men as sexual proclivity is an expected and accepted feature of their behaviour. The dichotomy of women as either Madonna or whore (Stanko, 1985), whereby the Madonna resists or refuses male sexual advances but the whore invites it, leads to the underlying notion that 'nice girls don't get raped' (Russell 1984, 1982). To refer again to Scully, she found that men would characterize *any* behaviour which violated gender role expectations as contributing to the commission of the act. The justification for rape would include reference to the woman's alleged reputation, as well as to whether or not she used drugs or alcohol. In many of the men's eyes these things meant that she had waived her rights to be treated with respect and therefore deserved what she got (Scully, 1990).

The potential for violence in commercial sex encounters can be seen as related more broadly to the structural position of women in this society. The fact that a woman is overtly selling sex in exchange for money or goods exacerbates the situation. In the first place a prostitute woman challenges male control by asserting her need to manage the encounter. In the second place a woman who prostitutes contravenes normative expectations of appropriate female behaviour. Pheterson makes the observation that prostitutes 'serve as models of female unchastity. As sexual solicitors they are assumed to invite male violence' (1988, p.225). A woman who prostitutes already violates norms of appropriate female behaviour and cannot be further violated. It is this model of thinking which asserts that prostitutes cannot be raped because of the work they do. In consequence male sexual violence against prostitute women can be and often is condoned. That these attitudes are prevalent in society is reflected in prostitutes' reluctance to report rape to the police (Silbert, 1981) as well as the reduced likelihood that such cases will be tried in court (Frohmann, 1991; Delacoste and Alexander, 1988).

In the following section a brief description of the research and the methods used for data collection is provided. The section after this presents background information on some of the streetworking prostitutes in this study and their conditions of work in the red light district. Following on from this is a brief description of the red light district in operation at night. This leads into a description of the processes by which sex is bought and sold. The conditions of work for streetworking prostitutes have an important bearing on the process of negotiating commercial sex and in turn the exercise of control in prostitute/client encounters.

Researching streetworking prostitution

This study of streetworking prostitution in Glasgow was set up in response to the uncertainty surrounding the link between prostitution and HIV spread, particularly in Europe and North America (Padian, 1987). It is a 3 year, Medical Research Council funded study which is both epidemiological and sociological in scope. The principal researchers are Neil McKeganey and myself.

Data were collected for this study through contacting prostitute women directly in the red light district during the times that they were working. In the first wave of data collection (January- September 1991) a total of 206 women were contacted by ourselves (McKeganey et al., 1992). Women thought to be prostituting were approached and, once appraised of our research identities, were offered assorted condoms, sterile injecting equipment, and a leaflet providing advice on local helping agencies and safer injecting practices. The ethical and methodological issues surrounding the mix of research and service provider roles have been detailed elsewhere (Barnard, 1992). Suffice to say that the incorporation of service provision into the research greatly facilitated the research since it allowed sustained contact with the women over time. It also did much to allay suspicion over possible motives for being in the area as well as providing a service which many women appeared to value.

Although the emphasis was on the collection of qualitative data it was also considered useful to collect quantitative data. To this end a sub-sample of 68 women contacted in the red light district were interviewed using a short standard instrument (McKeganey and Barnard, 1992). Some of this information is presented in the following section. These data cannot claim to

62

be representative but they do shed some light on the demographic characteristics of this population and their working practices.

The data provided here are largely derived from field diaries kept independently by the researchers. Data from interviews conducted with some of the women in their homes are also used. These interviews are semi-structured, often lasting upwards of an hour. Apart from the obvious advantage of having the time to cover issues in some depth, the women appear more inclined to reflect on the experience of prostitution than is usually the case whilst they are working. The interviews cover such issues as how prostitution is experienced, how client encounters are managed or not, and the impact prostitution has on relationships women have with their private partners, families and others, such as health practitioners.

Although the clients of prostitutes are also being contacted in this study, these data are only reported upon here to illustrate one specific point, given that the focus of the paper is on conditions of work for prostitutes. Clearly however, as the prostitute only represents one half of the equation in the commercial sex encounter, it is of at least equal importance to know something of the risk behaviours of the client population. The clients of prostitutes are being contacted in 2 genitourinary clinics in Glasgow, on the streets of the red light district, and by means of an advertisement placed in a national tabloid newspaper requesting clients to do a telephone interview (Barnard and McKeganey, 1992).

Some background information

The age range of the interviewed women was 16-51, the median age of the prostitutes was 24 years. The relatively young average age of these women is probably related to the high prevalence of injecting drug use in this population (71.6 per cent, a figure which compares with the overall estimate of 71.4 per cent of streetworking women in Glasgow [McKeganey et al., 1992]). In a community wide study of injectors in Glasgow the average age in 1990 was 24.1 (Frischer et al., 1992).

The median length of time that the prostitutes had worked was 2 years although the range in length of time that women had worked as prostitutes was considerable; from 2 weeks to 30 years. On average the women worked 5.2 nights a week and reported providing an average of 7.1 men with sexual services per night. As can be seen from the Table 4.1 below, oral sex was reportedly the most frequent sexual service provided. The second most frequent service provided was vaginal sex. Anal sex was not reported by any of the women in the sample (McKeganey and Barnard, 1992).

Table 4.1
Sexual services provided on the previous night
$n = 66$

Activity	Total	Average per woman
Vaginal sex	147	2.2
Oral sex	200	3.0
Anal sex	0	0
Masturbation	58	0.8

Of the 147 reported cases of vaginal sex provided on the previous night all but one involved the use of a condom. Two women reported not having used a condom for the provision of oral sex. Although the levels of condom use are high it is worthwhile pointing out that 18 of the women interviewed reported at least one condom failure in the last month worked.

Conditions of work for streetworking prostitutes

The red light district in Glasgow city centre comprises a well defined area of about eight streets. During the daytime it is primarily a business district. At night it is unambiguously concerned with the buying and selling of sexual services. Women can be seen standing alone or in pairs plying for business. Potential clients either drive or walk around the area. Women typically solicit men by asking them if they are 'looking for business'. Women also will look and nod to men in cars to engage their attention and from there negotiate with them over the possible provision of sexual services. Once agreement has been reached between prostitute and client they leave the immediate area. Sexual services are generally provided to clients in one of three settings: in cars; in one of the many nearby alleyways; or in the privacy of a flat or house. Deciding where to provide clients with sex was often a reflection of the women's concern for safety, particularly with regard to the provision of sex outside, as illustrated by the following extract from notes taken during field work:

> Kit said she really didn't like to go with punters into the alleys, she felt it was too dangerous. Annie responded to this saying that she didn't mind so long as the lane was near to a road and she could shout out to passers-by if she needed to. She said she liked to get punters who wore glasses so that if there was trouble she could use them to smash into the face of the punter.

The red light district is regularly policed. Although prostitution is not illegal, the activities associated with it such as soliciting are. Prostitutes expect to be picked up by police and fined by the courts on a relatively regular basis. The police appear to have adopted a regulatory role in their dealings with streetworking prostitutes. They maintain a watchfulness over the area and in particular are concerned to limit the potential for illegal activity such as drug dealing or violent crime such as robbery, rape, or assault. The red light district possesses a certain volatility which can flare up to create a tense and sometimes threatening atmosphere:

> Friday night and there is a really edgy atmosphere on the street, groups of loud, young males running up and down streets and darting into alleys. As we pass them I'm careful not to catch their eye. There are plenty of police cars - they seem to be looking for somebody since we've seen them racing up and down several streets and then sitting waiting in secluded alleys.

The following section considers the management of the commercial sexual encounter. Issues of power and control are considered as integral features of the interaction between prostitutes and clients.

Issues of control between prostitutes and clients

In traditional formulations of the heterosexual relationship there is a normative expectation of masculine dominance (Jackson, 1982; Richardson, 1990). Women are expected to adopt assenting, submissive roles particularly in their sexual relationships. From this perspective, the power balance is weighted in favour of the male. The prostitutes in this study however, did not represent their dealings with clients in this way. On the contrary, there appeared to be a strong occupational culture among the women which stressed the importance of female power in the commercial sexual encounter. This can perhaps be sensed in the following field extract where the woman concerned is commenting negatively on another woman's behaviour:

> Elaine pointed over to a woman who was just getting into the back of a car with two men. Initially we thought it was the fact there were two men which bothered her. She dismissed this saying she'd done business with them last night, 'but I went back to ma flat wi' them and there's always someone there.' It transpired that the problem was that the girl had not sat in the front passenger seat but in the back of a 2 door motor. 'You should never do that. See me I say, 'no' bein' cheeky but I wantae sit in the front,' that way if anything happens I

can kick the windae out. That Lindy got in the motor wi' 2 guys, she got in the back, I saw her, wait 'til she gets back here...'

Prostitutes generally assume an assertive stance with clients which is deliberately concerned with establishing the compliance of the client throughout the sexual encounter (Shedlin, 1990; Delacoste and Alexander, 1988). The women in this study accorded great importance to being in control of commercial sexual encounters. Their reasons for wanting control did relate to the practicalities of ensuring payment but also reflected an awareness of their vulnerability as women selling sex. 'Being in control' also took on the character of being a defensive action as the adoption of an assertive stance was a means of setting the terms of the interaction which hopefully the client would assent to and not try to subvert later on. The limited degree to which women were in control of clients was recognized by many and is evident in the words of the woman below:

If you're not in control of what you're doing then there's nae point doing it [prostitution]. I can only be in control of what I do to a certain extent because what I do is prostitution but you've got to feel in control to a certain extent.

The women's accounts of the negotiation process often reflected a preoccupation with establishing and retaining the initiative in dealing with clients. The comments made by the two women below are illustrative in this regard:

I was standing talking with a prostitute when a man slowly walked past. Seeing this the woman turned round and asked him if he were looking for business. He didn't appear to speak much English but he clearly was and asked about prices. 'Aye, well its £10 in a motor and £25 in a flat.' He said he had no car to which she replied 'It'll have to be in a lane then.' He then asked 'With or without Durex?' She didn't understand him at first, then she said 'Oh no, it'll have to be with Durex unless you wank yersel' off and I'll let you have a feel of me for £15.'

and:

I've got to put it across to them that I'm the one that's in charge and that's it. It's no' as if he's paying me for what he says he wants and he gets what he wants. I say, 'Well, what you want, well, that depends if I want to do that', you know what I mean? You get a lot of them that try [to take control], like they'll say, 'Wait a minute I'm payin' this money so I'll say what I want' sort of thing, but as long as you say to them, 'Look you're fucking payin' for ma time you're no

66

payin' for nothin' else' that's what I say. 'You pay for the time comin' from the town to the flat and from the flat to the town and the length of time that you're in the flat'. I say things like that if they try to get wide [wise] wi' me.

Once it is established that a man is seeking to buy sex, the prostitute begins the process of determining the price, the place, and the service on offer. As can be seen from the following field extract, there is a total absence of any emotional input. The explicit agenda is agreement on the terms of the transaction. In asserting these terms the woman takes charge of the situation:

Say you go over to the motor and you ask 'D'ye want business?' Or if it's a regular you just jump in wi' him, you know what the score is. Then you'll say 'Where are you wantin' it, in the car or in the flat?' And they'll say whichever, or they'll ask you how much it is or something. Like say they want the flat and then I'll say to him `What you wantin' in the flat?' He says sex, tell him how much it is, if he's wantin' oral tell him it's so much, if he's wantin' somethin' kinky I'll work out a price, or if he's wanting a certain length of time I'll work out a price.

At least part of the reason behind the deliberate adoption of a businesslike stance in dealing with clients is that it is an effective means of removing any ambiguity as to the true nature of the interaction in hand (Bloor et al., 1992). This is aptly demonstrated in the field extract below where the prostitute exposes the inappropriateness of the client's opening gambit:

As we talked with Marcie, a man crossed over the road and made over to talk to her. Holding an unlit cigarette he directly asked Marcie 'You got a light doll?' Without batting an eyelid she responded, 'Aye, and I don't do it outside by the way.' Whereas he had tried to initiate contact in terms more usual in noncommercial contacts - a pick up line in a disco perhaps she had immediately cut through all of that and established it firmly as a commercial contact.

Research into the processes leading up to the noncommercial heterosexual encounter suggests a deliberate lack of explicitness as to sexual intention, almost up to the point at which (penetrative) sex takes place (Wight, 1993; Kent et al., 1990). Prostitutes attempt to establish their contact with clients on a firmly commercial basis from the outset which entails that there be no such ambiguity as to the purposes of the meeting.

Prostitutes appear to feel that if the client acquiesces to her terms of business there is less of a likelihood for trouble. In the context of prostitution, trouble can take the form of robbery or rape or physical attack or worse. It is hardly surprising therefore, that prostitutes do all in their power to avoid such situations. In recognition of the potential dangers posed by clients, prostitutes seek to avoid men and situations which they judge to be personally dangerous. Two factors impinge importantly on the prostitute's ability to decide whether or not to take on a client, the first concerns knowledge of the client, the second concerns the amount of time available to make such decisions. It is in the nature of prostitution that many clients will be complete strangers to the women. The decision as to whether or not to go with any particular client must therefore be based on such minimal clues as whether or not they like the 'look' of the client (Delacoste and Alexander, 1988). A majority of the women interviewed reported that one of the main reasons for not agreeing to sex with a client in the last week worked was because they intuitively distrusted the man concerned. It is a measure of the women's vulnerability however, that in most cases these intuitive skills were all they had to go on.

> Karla said she trusted her intuition when deciding on whether or not to go with a client. 'The only thing you've got to go on is how you feel and if you don't feel safe there's nae point in going any further. When I first started I was naive and I didn't really know what was going on, I think the guys were in control 'cos they knew what happened whereas I didn't'. She contrasted this with the way she worked now.

The women appear to use a variety of ways to determine whether or not the client is safe to go with. Some women would base their judgement on the type of car the client drove; men in old, or cheap cars were often exampled as possibly untrustworthy. The women appear to watch their clients carefully, constantly assessing their behaviour and mannerisms. Women reported being uncomfortable with men who did not talk to them when they were in the car. For many women this was regarded as a bad sign:

> 'See when I get intae the motor, if somebody doesnae speak to me, if you're speaking to him and you're tryin' to get a conversation and he'll cut you off, well aye, that's it, I don't feel comfortable and I jus' get right out'. We then asked her what other signs she looked for. 'The way they look at ye. If you're sittin' and they're drivin' and they're no' talkin' that's one thing. But if you see they're drivin' and they're lookin' at ye fae the corner of their eye and they keep lookin' about themselves then that puts me off. To me I think they're dead shifty, you know what I mean?'

The worst scenario was where clients deliberately ignored instructions given by the woman regarding where she wanted to go with the client. This behaviour was taken by the women as clear indication that the client represented trouble and would result in them attempting to terminate the transaction:

> May was still really cross when we met up with her after having been messed around by two punters. Two men had wanted to buy sex from her and her friend. May had been uncertain, 'Y'know they looked dodgy, but she's goin' 'come on, a punter's a punter,' so I went.' She'd asked them to turn left at a turning, 'I was wantin' tae go to that wee car park. I know there were two of us and all but still...' Instead the car had carried right onto the motorway. At this point May said she'd demanded that they stopped the motor and she and her pal had got out and had to walk all the way back none the richer for their trouble.

The women clearly have very limited means of assessing the advisability of providing certain men with sexual services. For the most part they are reliant on their intuitive skills and experience. That these skills are by no means foolproof can be seen in the fieldnote below:

> Tina reported how she'd been attacked the other night. She'd gone with a man in a car. He'd attacked her in the car park. She was surprised at the attack. 'I always check them out and if they're dodgy I go 'oh, no, dodgy' and I don't go wi' them, but this one, he seemed dead plausible, y'know normal looking, quiet kind of guy, but when he was havin' sex he just started strangling me and biting ma neck.'

The second factor limiting the women's ability to screen out potentially violent, dangerous clients relates to the illegality of soliciting. This places a premium on the speedy curbside negotiation of the encounter so that prostitute and client can avoid attracting police attention (Lawrinson, 1991). This necessarily restricts the amount of time that can be spent negotiating such issues as safer sex but also importantly, weighing up the potential personal risks of getting into the car or going into a dimly lit alleyway.

Client bargaining power

There is not usually any shortage of men looking to buy the services of the prostitutes in the red light district. There are often large numbers of cars cruising the area, and there are also a number of men who approach the women on foot. This creates a position of some advantage for the streetworking women in their dealings with clients. However, the client represents income to the woman. This does place the client in the position of being able to negotiate over aspects of the sexual encounter. In prostitute and client negotiation there is potentially a certain tension between what the prostitute does or does not want to provide and what the client wants.

That prostitutes and clients do have potentially conflicting notions of the commercial sex contact can be seen from the interviews with the clients of female prostitutes. In the following two field extracts the men concerned clearly viewed the commercial transaction in somewhat different terms to those represented by the prostitutes. It is noticeable that, as potential buyers, they perceived themselves as occupying a strong bargaining position in the negotiation of the sexual act:

> Neil asked the man what attracted him to prostitution. 'Ah well it was the very fact that here were women who would do anything, you know, what it was that was required, you know, no bones about it, just that if they would do it they would charge for it, end of story.'

and:

> Neil wondered if part of the attraction of contacting a prostitute was that it was easier to ask her to do things than a partner. 'I suppose so, and the fact that you've got more dominance, i.e. you've got the money in your pocket then you've got the dominance over them.'

These data are used here illustratively as a means of indicating the degree to which the prostitute and the client might diverge in their conception of the dynamics of the commercial sexual encounter. The likelihood of conflict erupting between prostitute and client can perhaps best be seen as a latent tension.

From interviews with the women and also from field observations it appeared that, for the most part, the will of the prostitute prevailed. If clients wanted services that a woman was not prepared to provide she would break off negotiations at that point and leave the client to approach another woman. This can be seen in the following field extract:

> Tania commented that business was slow that evening. I asked if she'd done much, 'Just the one, two motors stopped but they were both wantin' it without condoms so I didnae go wi' them.'

Although the negotiation process between prostitutes and their clients is firmly commercial, not all services are on offer. Prostitutes would refuse to provide services which they felt impinged on their own sense of self-worth:

> Annie said she'd been asked by a punter to strip and provide him with oral sex in a lane. She had refused to do this saying to us, 'I've got ma pride, I'm no' gonnae be on ma knees for a tenner'.

However, it is also apparent that at least some women some of the time were prepared to compromise in order to reach agreement with clients. The classic example of this is where women agree to provide unsafe sex for extra money. Financial pressures may have an important influence on a woman's preparedness to agree to practices she might otherwise reject, particularly where she is working to finance a drug habit. For example, the woman in the field extract below was clearly very anxious to earn money:

> Kirsty (drug injector) had been telling us how little business there was in the town that night when she saw a man whom she thought might be a punter. However, Kate (another prostitute) was already in pursuit of him. Kirsty ignored her and cut across the road to ask him if he wanted business. We left at this point. A few moments later she shouted over to us to stop a white car that was waiting to cross the intersecting road. All night long she was chasing business, stopping any man who happened to be walking and almost flinging herself into passing cars.

The process of negotiation between prostitutes and clients does not appear to be fixed or static. Rather it can be seen to be highly dynamic and liable to change according to different contingencies and pressures. It is important to see both parties as involved in trying to achieve a vantage bargaining point. Prostitutes seek to capitalize on their position as vendors of a service that is in demand. Clients, on the other hand, represent monetary value to the women which gives them some advantage in negotiating sexual services. The relations prostitutes and clients establish with each other are not necessarily consensual since, as in business more generally, each party tries to achieve maximum benefit at minimum cost. There is a latent tension between clients and prostitutes which may or may not surface and may or may not be resolved. There is however, the potential for conflicting wants to lead to violent resolution by clients. It is this which prostitutes try to avoid through screening out clients they are uncertain of and through trying to manage the encounter.

The following section looks at those situations reported by the women where clients took control of the commercial encounter for their own, mostly violent, ends.

Violence and vulnerability

From contacts with the women it is apparent that most commercial sex encounters are unproblematic. Most clients are prepared to accede to the woman's terms of business. In addition, many women report having regular clients. The advantage of the regular client is that he is, for the most part, a known quantity. As the woman below commented:

> Ma regulars I know them, they're okay. I know what to expect. Some of ma regulars are okay guys, you know, to talk with and get along with, that's except for a few punters and like they're normally okay.

However, there are structural features of prostitution which create a position of advantage for the client. Prostitutes are vulnerable not simply because of the work they do but also because they have no necessary recourse to the law for protection. Prostitutes who encounter violent clients are most often obliged to respond individually to the threat posed to them.

Prostitutes report two main kinds of attack on them. These are rape and robbery. Some incidents involve both rape and robbery. Sometimes there is no apparent motive or rationale for attack beyond a desire for gratuitous violence:

> Walking along we heard a woman scream, we went up to the alleyway where the woman was standing. Her tights were ripped and her back wet with mud from where she'd fallen on her back. Apparently she'd been punched in the face by a man whom she was now watching walk slowly away up the alleyway. He started to run only when another prostitute and her boyfriend gave chase, later on we spoke to the prostitute who'd been attacked. She said he was a complete stranger and that he'd not taken anything from her. He'd told her he wanted business and once in the alley had just punched her full in the face and then walked off.

From the women's accounts it is apparent that rape by clients is not that unusual. Silbert (1981), in a study of attacks on prostitutes, found that 70 per cent reported having been raped in the preceding year. Clearly the potential always exists. A client could refuse to pay and then try to force the woman into providing sex. Not all women would define such situations as rape, as can be seen in the field extract below:

> Neil asked Cheryl if she'd ever been attacked by clients. 'Yeah, a few times, like most, I've had a few. You get punters all the time that try and get wise and not pay anything and just try and do business. Some people call it rape but I don't.' Neil wondered why she didn't call it rape. Cheryl replied 'Cos, I mean you're getting into a car to have sex with them. It depends, you know, they just want business without paying you. I mean I reckon I can handle myself okay and get the fuck out and just run. I mean obviously people are bigger and stronger than you. I had a bad experience just before I went off the

game there, well, I'd call this rape, 'cos it was very violent and I was, you know, he tried to do me in at the end of it.'

This woman appeared to define client rape situationally. The incident she defined as rape involved violent attack and, relatedly, the sense of being physically overpowered and not in control. Similarly, in the following field extract it is apparent that this woman holds herself responsible for the attack on her because she was too drunk to be in full command of her faculties:

At that time I went onto the drink really bad and I used to be drunk everytime I went up there (the town), so in a way I blame mysel' for not being alert enough. It was just as if like one minute he was alright and the next he was just ... It was 'I'm no' wearin' a condom' and I'm thinking okay. I mean, you know the change, you see it coming and well, give the guy what he wants and you'll get out his car. Well I blame it on the drink because ma reactions were that slow that when I went to open the door to get ma foot out he was 10 times quicker and he was over me and the hands round ma throat so I always blame mysel' more for that because of the drink. I wasnae alert enough.

It should however be noted that research on rape victims has consistently shown a tendency for women to blame themselves for being raped (Edwards, 1987; Tomaselli et al., 1986; Stanko, 1985). This is no less likely to be the case among female prostitutes, particularly given the importance that they attach to being in control of events.

It is precisely because of the threat of violence that prostitutes are highly attuned to issues of control in their relations with clients. It was apparent from many of the women's accounts that any deviation from the instructions given to clients about where to go and what to do immediately signalled potential danger. That these fears are clearly not unwarranted is demonstrated in the account below:

This guy comes' up me calling Sandy, that's the name I use down here, and since I don't really go wi' guys other than ma regulars who know me as Sandy, I thought he must be a regular. So I says to him 'Aye well you must know that I work up by the City Cross, you know away from the town' and so we're away in the motor and he doesn't turn up the way but fires onto the motorway. We ended up somewhere near the fruit market [out of town]. Then he started laying intae me, punching me and hittin' me and he raped me.' She also added that he'd stolen £75 or £85 from her. 'He tied me up with one of they big black bin bags, y'know the corporation bags. I had ma hands tied behind ma back and I was propped up against something. I don't know how I managed to loose ma hands free, I got out the way just as I saw he was in the motor and comin' towards me. He was gonnae run me over.'

In such situations the woman has little or no influence on the turn of events. In particular, a woman may be unlikely to secure client compliance to use a condom. In the above account the man had raped the woman without using a condom. Given the violence of the attack it seems highly likely that the woman's first concern was self-preservation rather than concern over the non-use of a condom. Nonetheless, the rape involved not only emotional trauma and physical damage but the potential for HIV transmission to take place as well as possible pregnancy. In the particular instance cited below the woman had been raped by two men, neither used a condom:

Last night I went with a punter in a motor. We parked and I did business wi' him for £20. Then this other bloke gets out the boot. They stole ma leather jacket, ma money and they raped me and they didnae wear a condom either so I'll have to go and get that AIDS test to see if I'm clear.

It is apparent that for all that streetworking prostitutes attempt to secure client compliance they remain fundamentally vulnerable. Many clients have the advantage of greater physical strength than the women added to which is the fact that prostitution often takes place in dimly-lit, deserted places. In this next section we will look at the range of strategies used by women to escape or mitigate such violent episodes.

Protective strategies

Prostitutes have only limited means of protecting against violent attack. The two main protective strategies open to prostitutes are firstly to screen out prospective clients they feel uncertain of, and secondly, to try to orchestrate the sexual encounter from beginning to end. By setting the agenda prostitutes aim to limit the potential for trouble or attack. However, whilst these measures provide important safeguards it is evident that they are not foolproof. In recognition of this many prostitutes reported the use of additional measures where possible. These involved the use of other women to watch out for them, the use of men as minders and recourse to weapons. Each of these measures has its problems both from a practical point of view and from the perspective of the police whose concerns lie with potential criminality.

It is not uncommon for two or more prostitutes to work co-operatively to protect against possible client attack. This may take the form of noting down car numbers (often deliberately in view of the client) or passing on descriptive information about clients known or thought to pose some kind of threat:

> As we walked over to Jane a car drew up. She went over to it but then came back and the car pulled away. I asked why she had not gone with him. 'I saw a notice put up by one of the other lassies in the drop-in [prostitute drop-in clinic] about some guy in a blue/black motor, a darkie, well he wasnae one he was a paki but still. And also they said something about an English accent. I thought when I walked over 'if he's got a Glasgow accent then I'll go wi' him' but he had an English accent so I left it.'

There were also women who attempted a more active form of protection as was the case in the field extract below:

> A woman we were talking to asked us to go down to the lanehead with her so as she could keep a watch on her friend who was in there with a punter. She says they always do this for each other and when they both have a punter will work the same lane. When one of them goes away in a motor the other takes a note of the car number plate and makes sure the man knows about it.

However, these measures can only ever be partially successful. The knowledge that a car number plate has been noted down may be reassuring in the sense that the woman could identify her attacker to the police but may not be sufficient to prevent the attack from happening. Similarly, even where two prostitutes try to keep a watch for the safety of the other it is inevitable that there will be situations where both women are with clients in different places. The reality for most streetworking prostitutes is that they work alone and if it comes to it, will probably also have to defend themselves against attack on their own.

Another strategy used by some women was to have men acting as minders for them. Glasgow streetworkers do not appear to have pimps as has been reported in other British cities like Birmingham (McLeod, 1982). Where women were using minders they were usually boyfriends or husbands. They would keep a watch on women's interactions with clients, keep hold of the money and on occasion follow them into the alleyway as well. This form of protection obviously has its uses:

> Janice had been working at 4 a.m. As it was so late her pal Colin had been there with her. She'd gone down an alleyway to give a guy oral sex for £10, Colin had stood at the lane head to look out for her. The client told her he'd recently been ripped off by another prostitute and so didn't want to pay until afterwards. 'I agreed to it, first time I ever

done it, stupid of me it was. Then at the end of it he goes 'I've nae money, I've only got £3.' So I called Colin over. He said 'Gonnae let us see your wallet aye?' But he said he didn't have a wallet so Colin just laid intae him then, we got his wallet off him, £95 it had in it. I wouldnae have taken it but that he started holdin' me up. If he'd of come out wi' the tenner he'd of saved all the bother.'

The police, however, actively discourage the practice of having minders present in the red light district since the presence of so many men in the area is an added source of tension and potential trouble. It was also the case that some women were reportedly using their partners less as minders than as a means of intimidating and robbing clients. More commonly perhaps, women spoke about the merits of having their partners at home when they took clients back. The knowledge that their partner was in the next room did appear to confer a sense of greater security upon the women:

Lisa said that she would refuse to go with a client to his flat but would work in her own place. 'Arnie's always there in the next room, nothing's gonnae happen wi' him around.'

The other means of self-defence used by some women was to carry a weapon or to have access to a weapon at home which could be used if necessary:

I've got a big hammer that I keep by the side of ma bed so if any punter starts trying anything on, he'll get what's what.

Again the police do not condone the practice of carrying a weapon, even for the purposes of self-defence since it can legally be construed as acting with intent to harm.

The range of measures prostitutes can employ as a means of further safeguarding against possible client attack are limited by practical and legal constraints. In effect, this means that prostitutes have to respond individually and with limited means to client threats or attacks. The paper concludes with a discussion of the range of policy initiatives which might arise out of the issues discussed here.

Conclusion and policy implications

Practically all of the women interviewed in this study had been confronted with violent clients on at least one occasion. Many women had been attacked by clients more than once. The frequency with which the women reported client violence indicated that there were certain structural features of prostitution which increased the likelihood of violence occurring. Closer inspection of the dynamics of the commercial sexual encounter suggest that it is fraught with issues of power and control. These may be made more acute by the fact that the women are actively asserting their intention to be in control of the transaction. In their overt adoption of such a role prostitutes directly contradict normative expectations of the sexually assenting and submissive female role.

However, prostitution itself appears to be an intrinsically risky activity since most commercial sex contacts are between strangers. Inevitably then, it contains a large element of unpredictability which cannot ever be wholly removed, despite the various means prostitutes use to try to decrease the likelihood of violence happening. The greater physical strength of most men relative to most women further places the women in a position of some disadvantage where clients become unco-operative or violent.

The prostitute/client encounter appears to contain within itself the potential for conflict which may or may not be resolved through violent means. However, these tendencies are probably further compounded by the illegalities associated with prostitution. Both prostitute and client are vulnerable to police arrest at the point at which they engage in negotiating the commercial sexual encounter. To avoid this eventuality negotiations are usually brief and hurried. Clearly the compressed time available does not assist the process of deciding whether or not the client is safe to go away with. The laws which govern prostitution ensure that for the most part the provision of sexual services has to be clandestine. This means that they are often with men in dark alleyways, deserted car parks, or empty flats. In such situations the women have to rely upon their own wits, they cannot anticipate help. By forcing the practice of prostitution underground the dangers associated with the sale of sex are further exacerbated.

The existing laws regulating prostitution inevitably hamper the development of policies which could lessen the incidence of violence against prostitutes. A first small step however, might be for recognition of the many dangers faced by prostitutes. It is an interesting, if telling, observation that most of the impetus for the legalization of female prostitution has been motivated by a concern for the better regulation and control of the trade. Most recently this concern has been activated by fears that prostitutes will act as a conduit for HIV infection to spread in the general population. Little equivalent attention has been paid to the possible reasons why prostitutes *themselves* might benefit from some relaxation of the legal restrictions on prostitution. Whilst the dynamics of the commercial sexual encounter are, in themselves, replete with issues of power and control, the vulnerability of prostitutes to client attack is increased by current legislation on prostitution.

It is highly probable that the legal restrictions on prostitution will remain in force for the foreseeable future. This being so, there are good grounds for the implementation of policies aimed at minimizing the likelihood of violence. One way might be to capitalize on the large stock of knowledge the prostitutes have about men in the area. In Glasgow for example, the local drop-in clinic for streetworking prostitutes (Carr et al., 1992) has a notice board where women can paste descriptive warnings about particular men in the area. Clearly such measures are most likely to succeed where there are premises for the use of prostitutes.

A more direct approach to the problem of client violence would be to designate places where women could take clients. In one city in the Netherlands for example, a car park has been provided for the use of prostitutes and clients. It is well lit and frequented by other women, both of these factors help to reduce the likelihood of trouble (Kleinegris, 1991). However, such a measure is made possible by the decriminalization of prostitution in certain parts of many Dutch cities. There are obstacles to the implementation of similar facilities in Britain given the obvious contradictions between such a measure and the legal status of prostitution. In this regard it could be pointed out that the provision of drop-in facilities in many UK cities is also somewhat in opposition to the current legal situation, nonetheless there have been compelling policy arguments for their implementation. In recognizing the many dangers inherent in prostitution perhaps policy makers may be better placed to argue for the provision of means to reduce the likelihood of client violence.

In many senses prostitutes are easy targets for men who have violent inclinations. This is not only because it is in the nature of their work to go with strangers to oftentimes dark, lonely places. It is also the case that prostitutes are treated as second class citizens because the work they do is considered by many to be immoral as well as illegal. A very likely consequence of this is that some men feel able to physically intimidate women without fear of reprisal. In the first place many women do not report violent attacks by men to the police because they doubt that they will be taken seriously (Silbert, 1981; Delacoste and Alexander, 1988). Frohmann (1991), in a study of prosecutor's decisions to reject trying rape cases in court, found that victim credibility was a major factor influencing their decisions. The fact of being a prostitute is likely to have an important bearing on the credibility accorded the woman's allegations. Those few women in this study who had taken a case to court reported that from the point when they were identified as prostituting the case had gone against them. Secondly, the decision to take the case to court to try to secure a conviction requires that the woman confront the stigma of being labelled a common prostitute.

There exists a perception that prostitutes who are attacked do in some way deserve it because of the work that they do. In this sense there are undoubtedly those who would argue that prostitutes cannot get raped since they are in the business of providing sex anyway.

Perhaps men who see prostitutes as easy targets would be discouraged from this perception if there were more successful convictions of other men who attack prostitutes. This could be achieved if the police made a concerted attempt firstly, to encourage women to report all such instances by taking them seriously and secondly, to adopt a policy of vigorous pursuit of such men. Beyond this however, there remains the need for a sea change in the public perception of prostitutes as second class citizens who do not qualify for the same civil liberties as the rest of the population.

Acknowledgements

I owe thanks to Neil McKeganey, both because these data were collected with him and because of the time and effort he has put into commenting on this paper. I am also grateful to Mick Bloor and Jenny Kitzinger for valuable comment. I thank the Medical Research Council for their financial support of this study. In addition I would like to thank Dr Laurence Gruer and Dr Susan Carr as well as representatives of Strathclyde Regional Police for their assistance. Lastly but by no means least thanks are due to the many women who agreed to be part of this research.

The Public Health Research Unit is funded by the Chief Scientist Office of the Scottish Home and Health Department and the Greater Glasgow Health Board. The opinions expressed in this paper are not necessarily those of the Scottish Home and Health Department.

Bibliography

Barnard, M. (1992), 'Working in the dark: researching female street prostitution' in Roberts, H. (ed.), *Women's Health Matters*, Routledge, London.

Barnard, M. and McKeganey, N. (1992), *Risk behaviours among a sample of male clients of female prostitutes*, VIII International Conference on AIDS/III STD World Congress, Amsterdam, poster (PoC 5062).

Bloor, M., McKeganey, N., Finlay, A. and Barnard, M. (1992), 'The inappropriateness of psycho-social models of risk behaviour for understanding hiv-related risk practices among glasgow male prostitutes', *AIDS Care*, Vol. 4, No. 2, pp. 131-7.

Carr, S., Green, D., Goldberg, D., Cameron, J., Gruer, L. et al. (1992), 'HIV prevalence among street prostitutes attending a health-care drop-in clinic in Glasgow', *AIDS*, Vol. 6, No. 12, pp. 1553-4.

Chesler, Phyllis (1978), *About Men*, Simon and Schuster, New York.

Clark, L. and Lewis, D. (1977), *Rape: The Price of Coercive Sexuality*, The Women's Press, Toronto.

Cohen, J.B. (1989), 'Overstating the risk of AIDS: scapegoating prostitutes', *Focus, A Guide to AIDS Research*, Vol. 4, pp. 1-2.

Delacoste, Frederique and Alexander, Priscilla (1988), *Sex Work: Writings by Women in the Sex Industry*, Virago Press, London.

Dobash, R. Emerson and Dobash, R. (1979), *Violence Against Wives: A Case Against the Patriarchy*, Open Books, London.

Dobash, R.P., Dobash, R. Emerson, Wilson, M. and Daly, M. (1992), 'The myth of sexual symmetry in marital violence', *Social Problems*, Vol. 39, No. 1, pp. 71-85.

Edwards, S. (1987), "Provoking her own demise': from common assault to homicide' in Hamner, J. and Maynard, M. (eds.), *Women, Violence and Social Control*, Macmillan Press, Basingstoke.

Evason, Eileen (1982), *Hidden Violence: A Study of Battered Women in Northern Ireland*, Farset Co-operative Press, Belfast.

Faugier, J., Hayes, C. and Butterworth, C. (1992), *Drug Using Prostitutes, Their Health Care Needs And Their Clients*, Final Report to the Department of Health, London.

French, Dawn (1990), *Working: My Life As A Prostitute*, Gollancz Pub., London.

Frischer, M., Bloor, M., Green, S., Goldberg, D., Covell, R. et al. (1992), 'Reduction in needle sharing among a community-wide sample of injecting drug users', *International Journal of STD and AIDS*, Vol. 3, pp. 288-90.

Frohmann, L. (1991), 'Discrediting Victim's Allegations Of Sexual Assault: Prosecutorial Accounts Of Case Rejections', *Social Problems*, Vol. 38, No. 2, pp. 213-26.

Green, E., Hebron, S. and Woodward, D. (1987), 'Women, leisure and social control' in Hamner, J. and Maynard, M. (eds.) *Women, Violence and Social Control*, Macmillan Press, Basingstoke.

Hamner, Jalna and Maynard, Mary (1987), *Women, Violence and Social Control*, Macmillan Press, Basingstoke.

Holland, J., Ramazanoglu, C., Scott, C., Sharpe, S. and Thomson, R. (1992), 'Risk, power and the possibility of pleasure: young women and safer sex', *AIDS Care*, Vol. 4, No. 3, pp. 273-283.

Horowitz, R. (1981), 'Passion, submission and motherhood: the negotiation of identity by unmarried inner city Chicanas', *The Sociological Quarterly*, Vol. 22, pp. 241-52.

Jackson, S. (1982), *Childhood and Sexuality*, Basil Blackwell, Oxford.

James, A. (1986), 'Learning to belong: the boundaries of adolescence' in Cohen, A. (ed.), *Symbolising Boundaries: Identity and Diversity in British Cultures*, Manchester University Press, Manchester.

Kleinegris, M. (1991), *Innovative AIDS prevention among drug-using prostitutes*, paper presented to Second International Conference on the Reduction of Drug Related Harm, Barcelona.

Lawrinson, S. (1991), *Prostitutes And Safe Sexual Practice*, Paper presented at British Sociological Association Annual Conference, Manchester.

McKeganey, N. and Barnard, M. (1992), 'Selling sex: female street prostitution and HIV risk behaviour in Glasgow', *AIDS Care*, Vol. 4, No. 4, pp. 395-407.

McKeganey, N., Barnard, M., Leyland, A., Coote, I. and Follet, E. (1992), 'Female street-working prostitution and HIV infection in Glasgow', *British Medical Journal*, Vol. 305, pp. 801-4.

McLeod, E. (1982), *Women Working: Prostitution Now*, Croom Helm, London.

Padian, N. (1987), 'Heterosexual transmission of Acquired Immunodeficiency Syndrome: international perspectives and national projections', *Review of Infectious Diseases*, Vol. 9, pp. 947-59.

Pheterson, G. (1988), 'The social consequences of unchastity' in Delacoste, F. and Alexander, P. (eds.), *Sex Work: Writings by Women in the Sex Industry*, Virago Press, London.

Richardson, D. (1990), 'AIDS education and women: sexual and reproductive issues' in Aggleton, P., Davies, P. and Hart, G. (eds.), *AIDS: Individual, Cultural and Policy Dimensions*, Falmer Press, Brighton.

Russell, Diane (1984), *Sexual Exploitation*, Sage Publications, London.

Russell, Diane (1982), *Rape in Marriage*, Macmillan, New York.

Sanday, P. (1986), 'Rape and the silencing of the feminine' in Tomaselli, S. and Porter, R. (eds.), *Rape*, Basil Blackwell, Oxford.

Scully, Diane (1990), *Understanding Sexual Violence: A Study of Convicted Rapists*, Harper Collins, London.

Shedlin, M. (1990), 'An ethnographic approach to understanding HIV high-risk behaviours: prostitution and drug abuse' in Leukefeld, C.G., Battjes, R.J. and Amsel, Z. (eds.), *AIDS and Intravenous Drug Use: Community*

Intervention and Prevention, Hemisphere Publishing Corporation, New York.

Silbert, Mimi (1981), *Sexual Assault of Prostitutes*, Delancey Street Foundation, San Francisco.

Stanko, Elizabeth (1985), *Intimate Intrusions: Women's Experiences of Male Violence, Rape, Child Sexual Abuse and Sexual Harassment*, Routledge, London.

Synn-Stern, L. (1992), 'Self-injection education for street level sexworkers' in O'Hare, P., Newcombe, R., Matthews, A., Buning, E. and Drucker, E. (eds.), *The Reduction of Drug-Related Harm*, Routledge, London.

Tomaselli, Sylvana and Porter, Roy (1986), 'Introductory Chapter' in Tomaselli, S. and Porter, R. (eds.), *Rape*, Basil Blackwell, Oxford.

Wight, D. (1993), 'Boys' thoughts and talk about sex in a working class locality of Glasgow', *Sociological* Review, Vol. 42, No. 4, pp. 703-37.

5 Violence in the United States

Billie Weiss

Introduction

Former Surgeon General, C. Everett Coop has said that 'The professions of medicine, nursing, and the health-related social services must come forward and recognize violence as their issue and one that profoundly affects the public health' (Rosenberg et al., 1991). The epidemic of violence in America is a public health crisis of epic proportions.

Americans take pride in espousing a social contract that respects the rights of individuals, promotes equality, and values the sanctity of life. The history of the United States began with a violent and bloody revolution. American heroes are traditionally violent. Violence permeates American society. Part of the American tradition lies in glorifying the violent past, and the present. American children learn that the West was won by violence and many Americans believe that it is their right be armed, despite the fact that studies show that a firearm is more likely to be used against the owner or the owner's family than to defend oneself (Kellerman et al., 1993). Despite the perception of an American Dream of peace and harmony, more people are killed by violence in the United States than any other industrialized country in the world, and the majority of these homicides are committed with a firearm. Violence so permeates American society that many believe that it is an immutable part of the human condition.

Nationally, more than 30,000 people die each year as a result of violence (Kellerman et al., 1993). Each year in the United States, approximately 20,000 persons die from homicide, and a similar number die from suicide (Rosenberg et al., 1991; Baker et al., 1992). Homicide is the fourth leading cause of death for children between one and fourteen years of age, and ranks second for ages fifteen to twenty four. Among African Americans fifteen to thirty-four years of age, it is the leading cause of death (Baker et al., 1992). If all Americans died at the same rate as young African American men, approximately 260,000 persons would die from homicide each year (F.B.I., 1993). For infants less than one year of age excluding the perinatal period, homicide is the leading cause of death as a result of injury (Waller, 1985). Homicide rates are highest for young men between the ages of 15 and 34 years. It is estimated that firearms are responsible for 60-80 per cent of the homicides in the United States. The United States leads all countries in the industrialized world in homicide deaths.

Table 5.1
Homicide rates for males, all ages, 1989-1990 by country
All rates are deaths per 100,000 population

U.S. Black	65.6
U.S. All	15.5
U.S. White	8.6
Scotland	4.0
Hungary	3.8
Canada*	2.9
Portugal	2.4
Austria	1.9
Switzerland	1.4
Denmark	1.2
Japan	0.7
England & Wales	0.6

Source: WHO Annual and National Center for Health Statistics
             *1989 only

In public health, injuries are defined by the notion of intentionality (see chapter 1). Unintentional injuries are those events previously described as accidents, such as drowning, falls and motor vehicle crashes. Intentional injuries include homicides, assaults, suicides and those resulting from legal intervention by the police or armed forces. Problems arise with deriving a definition based on intentionality. Public health records such as death certificates, hospital discharge data, and coroners' reports do not record intentionality with the exception of completed suicides and homicide. Given that intentionality cannot be established, fatal injury rates are most often used as a proxy to describe the epidemiology of injuries in general, and intentional injuries in particular. The cause of an injury is most often described by the mechanism of the injury or the external cause of the injury. For violent injuries the mechanism of injury is primarily the means or method causing the injury, so that the weapon involved in violence is similar to the vector of disease. Increasingly the vector of violence in the United States is a gun, primarily a handgun (Smith and Laurman, 1988). The importance of firearms, particularly handguns, in the alarmingly high homicide rates in the United States is further emphasized when deaths due to handguns are compared with those in other industrialized nations.

Deaths caused by firearms are classified as intentional, unintentional, and those due to legal intervention. Intentionality is most often determined by a coroner's investigation and/or law enforcement agencies.

The classification of unintended firearm injuries raises the issue of whether a device whose only purpose is to kill can ever be classified as being used unintentionally. During a statistically average day in the United States, one child dies from an unintentional shooting. So-called accidental shootings are the third leading cause of death for 10-29 year olds and the fifth leading cause of death for children from 1-15 years of age. Fifty per cent of all unintentional child shootings occur in the victim's home and an additional 40 per cent occur in the home of a friend or relative (Fingerhut, 1994). In many parts of the United States, suicide rates exceed those for homicides. In 1990, of the 37,184 Americans killed with a firearm, 51 per cent (18,964) committed suicide, and in 1991 48.4 per cent of the 38,235 deaths due to a firearm were classified as suicide (Fingerhut, 1990). In many urban areas however, such as Los Angeles, California, deaths due to interpersonal violence exceed those due to self-inflicted violence. The common element in both types of violence is the availability of a gun, which escalates suicidal thoughts into a fatal reality and, in the case of most homicides, a dispute into a fatal outcome. In order to understand the epidemiology of violent injuries and the magnitude of the escalating epidemic, it is necessary to measure and understand the non-fatal injuries as well. The data regarding non-fatal violent events must rely on a multiplicity of data sources which are not necessarily compatible, such as public health records and criminal justice system records. Non-fatal violence is often under-reported due to difficulties in collecting standardized data. Information on non-fatal domestic violence, child abuse, elder abuse, is often unrepresentative of the levels in the general population, since investigators must rely on studies which do not, and often cannot, select an unbiased sample. Therefore results may not always be applicable to the general population.

Public health records focus on the victim and criminal justice records focus on the perpetrator, and the two are rarely integrated. Available records do not always report intentionality, which may skew the data on intentional violence to give a false interpretation of the magnitude of the problem. In public health, homicide is used as a surrogate measure for all categories of interpersonal violence, since it is an obvious outcome and reporting is relatively complete. Using homicide as the indicator for monitoring trends and changes in the epidemiology of interpersonal violence permits analysis of trends and comparisons locally, nationally, and internationally.

Victims of homicide

The profile of homicide victims throughout the industrialized world is similar. Worldwide rates are highest for males from 15 to 34 years of age. The United States leads all countries in the industrialized world in homicide rates, by a magnitude of more than 100. In the United States, rates vary by age, gender, racialised and ethnic group. In addition, homicide rates vary by geographic location. Young ethnic minority men aged between 15 and 34 years have rates three times higher than other groups.

Table 5.2
Deaths due to handguns in 1992, by country

Australia	13
Great Britain	33
Sweden	36
Japan	60
Switzerland	97
Canada	128
United States	13,220

Source: Handgun Control Inc., Washington DC

The public health approach to combating violence

The public health approach to violence is a concept that has been developed over the past ten years or so, as it has become increasingly clear that the numbers of deaths and years of potential life lost due to violence is unacceptably high. The epidemic of violence has claimed more lives in Los Angeles than AIDS since 1981, and has required more person-hours of attention from practioners in emergency departments and rehabilitation centers than any other single cause. The public health approach to violence is similar to that used with tobacco use. The ultimate goal of this approach is preventing the occurrence of violence by using primary prevention strategies.

Such an approach involves changing the perception of what is normal or acceptable behaviour. Violence and the injuries that result from violent behaviour are classified as part of the general topic of injury epidemiology and injury prevention.

Despite the fact that most people associate epidemiology with infectious diseases, injury as a public health issue is not new. The public health approach to preventing injuries generally is directed toward interventions that are known to be effective. For example, such an approach to automobile passenger injuries involves the use of passive protection devices, such as seat belts and air bags, and health education to stress the importance of using seat belts and child passenger safety seats. Other examples of the public health model include the use of smoke detectors and the use of barrier fences between house and backyard swimming pool.

It is appropriate to address violence as a public health issue on two counts: it is a measurable phenomenon; and there are appropriate and effective prevention and intervention strategies with which violence has been shown to be preventable. In order to understand the preventive approach it is necessary to understand where primary, secondary, and tertiary prevention fit into the model. Primary prevention is where most public health efforts are directed and aims to prevent exposure to violence and behaviours that lead to violence. Primary prevention may be thought of in the same way as immunization in a medical model. Primary strategies to prevent domestic violence and child abuse would include: provision of parenting training, provision of violence prevention training for pre-school children and their families, teaching conflict resolution skills, mentoring programs and dispute mediation in schools. Secondary prevention focuses on diversion and intervention after exposure to risk factors, for instance, probation programs for those who have been involved in high risk behaviours. Such programs focus on diverting young gang members from engaging in violent gang behaviour, and one of the best examples is the organization of midnight basketball for gang members. In the medical model secondary prevention involves treatment of an illness. Law enforcement is the most common provider of tertiary prevention of violence. It is after the fact and aims to prevent repeated violence. In the medical model, tertiary prevention is the rehabilitative phase of the intervention whose goal is to stop the spread of the disease or the epidemic. Obviously, there are some differences and discrepancies between the medical model and the public health model of violence prevention, but the use of the model provides an example of a measurable, predictable, preventable epidemic, which can be successfully addressed by a comprehensive public health approach. A public health approach has successfully changed behaviour regarding the use of tobacco, and sexual behaviour has been changed as part of the strategy to prevent the spread of AIDS.

Primary prevention is assumed to be the preferable strategy because of the long term hope for change that it offers. In common with the spread of HIV and widespread tobacco use, the costs of violent behaviour in terms of mortality are high and the secondary and tertiary preventative strategies available are ineffective compared with primary prevention.

Urban versus rural violence

Homicide rates are highest in urban areas, which often leads to the assumption that most violence is the result of random street violence. A study by Fingerhut and Kleinman (1989) compared rates for core counties (containing primary central cities with populations greater than or equal to 1,000,000), fringe counties (primarily suburban counties with populations of at least 1,000,000), medium counties (with populations between 250,000 and 999,999), small counties (with populations of less than 25,000), and non-metropolitan counties. They found that among black male teenagers 72 per cent of the homicides in this group occurred in a metropolitan core county, compared with 6 per cent in non-metropolitan areas. The authors of this study compared death rates for firearm homicides, motor vehicle injury and all natural causes for core counties and non-metropolitan counties in 1988 and computed rate ratios for the urban and rural counties. They found that the firearm homicide rates showed the greatest rate ratios for both black and white teenagers (ratios of 10.8 and 4.9 respectively). Motor vehicle injuries, by contrast, showed a reverse relationship between core and non-metropolitan counties with ratios for both blacks and whites of 0.5. All natural causes of death showed no difference between urban and rural areas (Fingerhut and Kleinman, 1989).

Even in cities, with the highest homicide rates, the majority of homicides and assaults are due to relationships, arguments, and the easy availability of a firearm. The majority of homicides (estimates range from 60 per cent (Weiss, 1994) to 80 per cent (Baker et al., 1992)) occur among people who know each other. Substance abuse, including alcohol and other drugs, play a major contributing role in escalating anger into homicide. The role of firearms, particularly handguns, in escalating the epidemic cannot be overstated. Increasing homicide rates parallel increasing availability of firearms, including handguns (Wintemute, 1994). Handguns are most often associated with urban violence, and long guns such as rifles are more often associated with rural homicide.

Rates of homicide are higher in under-served, impoverished communities (Weiss, 1993). Communities with high rates of poverty and unemployment are also communities with large ethnic minority populations. While minority ethnicity is often identified as a risk factor for violent victimization, minority ethnicity may not be an indicator of risk as much as deprived social class and poverty. Studies that have examined injury rates by ethnicity and poverty have shown that when ethnic group is held constant, the same communities remain at risk from violence, indicating that poverty may play at least as important a role as ethnic group (Chang et al., 1992).

Although rates of homicide are greater in under-served urban areas and fatal outcomes are reported at a lower rate in rural areas, family violence and relationship violence may be nonetheless prevalent in rural settings. Biased reporting and lack of case ascertainment may greatly underestimate the magnitude of the problem in rural settings. Available data suggest that in rural areas rates of self-inflicted violence are higher than that caused by interpersonal relationships. Further investigation is needed to document the variance in rates of violent injury between urban and rural settings.

Youth violence

Youthful street gangs are not a new phenomenon. A brief review of the literature regarding the history of gangs shows that in 19th century London, youthful street gangs terrorized the residents. Prior to the United States Civil War, it was reported that New York City had approximately 30,000 street gang members. At other times Philadelphia and Chicago were proclaimed to be gang capitals. Currently it is thought that Los Angeles is the street gang capital of the world (Garcetti, 1992). In the United States a recorded history of gang activity indicates that second and third generation gang members exist in many urban areas of the country. In Los Angeles, it is estimated that there are more than 100,000 gang members, who belong to more than 1,000 gangs (McBride, 1993). Youth gang behaviour parallels the stages of adolescent development: the need to associate with peers; to fit in; to break away from home; not only typify gang behaviour, but the middle stage of adolescence as well. It is not the gangs themselves that are a menace so much as the violent and criminal behaviour in which they often indulge. The increase in gang violence is traced to the accessibility and availability of firearms, including high-tech automatic and semi-automatic weapons. The easy access to drugs is likely to have increased the lethality of gang violence. Illegal activity is far from the only reason why youths join gangs. Members of gangs commit more types of crime (and more frequently) than non-gang youth, yet many gang members are not involved in crime. Most gang members are not involved in drug trafficking and most Los Angeles gangs are not organized drug distribution rings. Most gangs are loosely knit, with several members who fill leadership roles, depending on their age and situation. Membership fluctuates and gang members have varying degrees of commitment to the gang. Gang cohesiveness is highest when the gang is challenged by other groups or outsiders (McBride, 1993).

Drive-by shootings and other gun related activities by gang members have increased as guns on the streets have proliferated. Drive-by killings are a direct result of the availability of firearms. People injure people; guns kill people (Genelin, 1992). Gang related homicides in Los Angeles in 1992 were four times higher than the comparable figures for 1978. However, the annual totals for gang related homicides decreased in 1981, 1982, 1984, and 1993.

Table 5.3
Gang related homicides as a percentage of total homicides in Los Angeles County

Year	Total Homicides	Number Gang Related Homicides	Percent Gang Related Homicides
1980	1,825	351	19.2
1981	1,661	292	17.6
1982	1,511	205	13.6
1983	1,480	216	14.6
1984	1,438	212	14.7
1985	1,463	271	18.5
1986	1,542	328	21.3
1987	1,553	387	24.9
1988	1,522	452	29.7
1989	1,766	554	31.4
1990	1,964	690	35.1
1991	2,062	771	37.4
1992	2,209	803	36.4
1993	2,067	724	35.0

There are difficulties in comparing rates of gang activity worldwide or even within the United States, since the definition of a gang member is subject to interpretation. The Los Angeles Police Department defines a gang as a group of three or more persons who have a common identifying sign or symbol and whose members individually or collectively engage in criminal activity, creating an atmosphere of fear and intimidation within the community (Jackson, 1992). The Sheriff's Department uses a similar definition, but definitions vary by locality and police agency. Gang related crimes are also subject to interpretation by geographic location. The Los Angeles Police Department defines gang related crimes as those in which at least one identified active or associate gang member is the criminal, the victim, or both. Gang reported crimes include assault with a deadly weapon, attempted murder, shooting at an inhabited dwelling, and homicide. Several studies have attempted to test the reliability of reporting methods (Maxson and Kline, 1990; Meehan and O'Carroll, 1992). These studies have affirmed that the Los Angeles Police Department gang related homicide classification was found to be consistent 'between cases, between investigators, between stations, and over time' (Meehan and Kline, 1990). Predominant characteristics of gang related homicide in Los Angeles (1989 to 1991) included disproportionately high numbers of black, male victims. Ninety two per cent of all victims were male and 95 per cent of the victims were either Hispanic or black. This compares with population proportions of Hispanics and blacks at 40 per cent and 13 per cent respectively, so as a proportion of victims of gang violence these figures constitute a considerable over-representation. Eighty-six per cent of the victims were between the ages of 15 and 34 years of age.

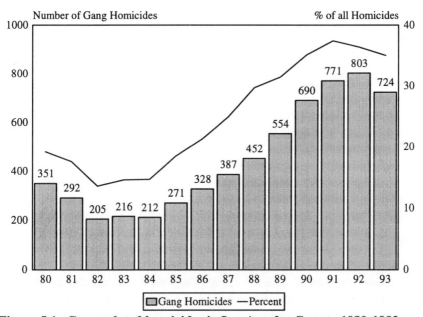

Figure 5.1 Gang related homicides in Los Angeles County 1980-1993
Source: Los Angeles County Department of Health Services Injury and Violence Prevention Program, December 1994

Among the gang homicide victims studied, 58 per cent were gang members killed by other gang members and 42 per cent were non gang members, or innocent bystanders (Gustafson et al., 1992). In Los Angeles approximately two-thirds of all homicides are firearm related (LACDHSIVPP, 1992); among gang homicides, however, 88 per cent of the homicides were firearm related. Eighty-four per cent of the time a handgun was the weapon of choice for the gang related homicides.

As with all homicides, the victim and perpetrators are most often of the same age, ethnicity and gender. It is often assumed that gang related homicide can be tied to drugs and alcohol. However, this is in fact difficult to substantiate for a number of reasons: law enforcement records only report a homicide as gang and drug related if the homicide is the direct result of a 'drug deal'; gang related homicide victims are not consistently tested for drugs and alcohol at autopsy; and finally, suspects are not always apprehended at the scene of the crime and testing for drugs and alcohol at the time of arrest may not reflect conditions at the time of the crime (Weiss and Strassburg, 1992).

The influence of street gangs has spawned a number of high risk behaviours among youth. There is great concern in the increased reporting of children carrying guns to school. In Los Angeles alone, the number of public school children expelled for carrying a firearm to school has increased almost 200 per cent within the past ten years. Approximately two-thirds of the 2,000 children expelled from public schools each year in Los Angeles County are expelled for carrying a gun to school. The Center for Disease Control has estimated that 20 per cent of young people have carried a firearm to school at least once.

Reliance on incarceration to control such activity has glamourized the gang 'life style' and may contribute to the proliferation of youthful street gangs. As law enforcement activity has escalated to control gangs, violence has increased concomitantly. Emphasis on long term solutions is largely ignored in the climate of 'three strikes you're out'. Isn't it about time that we looked at successful prevention models?

The media

In recent years there has been much discussion about the media's role in community violence. Does constant exposure to television violence anaesthetize the population to the horror of violence? Is the media a mirror or an inventor of community lifestyles? The nightly news sensationalizes violence and brings a mythical perception of the amount and type of violence in our communities. The escalating fear factor that has prompted the increased 'arming' of our homes can be in part, traced to the influence of the media. It has become increasingly clear that Americans are more likely to respond to the sight of children dying in places such as Somalia, Sarejevo, and Rwanda than they are to the deaths of their own children through violence. This contradiction can be explained in part, by the way in which the media represents violence in foreign countries, compared with their representation of violence in the United States.

Media coverage of children dying by violent means in countries throughout the world focuses on the victims, thus generating sympathy for the victims and their families. Conversely, the nightly news in the United States focuses on the perpetrators of the violence in the United States, thus eroding concern for the victim and enhancing fear of the perpetrators. This focus on the perpetrator instead of the victim has contributed to the 'lock-em-up' philosophy so prevalent in the national policy of the United States at the present time. This policy continues despite the fact that the United States incarcerates a larger proportion of the population than any other industrialized country, yet the rate of violence continues to escalate. Incarceration without treatment and rehabilitation thus fails as a preventative measure against violence.

The public health approach to prevention

A public health response to the crisis caused by violent injuries requires a comprehensive public health approach. The public health model includes primary, secondary, and tertiary prevention. Violence and violent behaviour follows a similar pattern to other recent public health epidemics. Its occurrence can be measured and monitored; groups at increased risk and high risk behaviours can be identified. Therefore, the adverse outcomes associated with the epidemic can be predicted and prevented. A public health approach to violence prevention begins with education to increase public awareness about the issue, and about high risk behaviours that can be changed to reduce the risk of becoming a victim of violence. Primary prevention requires a long term commitment and a comprehensive effort from all segments of the community, including the individual.

There have been successful community violence prevention programmes, for instance Jordan High School in the Watts section of Los Angeles. A problem in attempting to replicate these successful community based programs and school curricula is a lack of systematic evaluation for program effectiveness. Such a lack often limits the opportunity to replicate programs. Systematic evaluation allows successful programs to build and expand among vulnerable populations and would encourage funders to provide resources for long term program support. Evaluation is crucial to demonstrate effectiveness of primary, secondary, and tertiary prevention models. Unfortunately comprehensive evaluation is expensive. Most funding agencies limit access to effective evaluation by funding programs and evaluations for 3 to 5 years. Long term follow-up for evaluation may take 10 to 15 years to determine long term effectiveness.

In addition to discussing the progress of community programs that provide mentoring, tutors and after school activities, teaching parenting skills to adults and youths, and encouraging community input into community program development, professionals must be trained in dispute mediation, conflict resolution, and alternative methods for dealing with anger and cultural sensitivity. Training for medical providers, mental health providers, teachers, and public agencies is crucial to changing community norms to promote the concept that violence is preventable.

Community coalition building for prevention

The public health model requires broad based support from the entire community, including public and private agencies, governmental agencies, the media, schools, university research, medical providers (public and private), law enforcement, probation, the judicial system, emergency medical systems, social services, and the community. A comprehensive community coalition shows the greatest promise for promoting effective violence prevention. A broad based effort requires that we do not address violence by category, but rather by its root causes of poverty, drugs, lack of self empowerment. It seems intuitive that a prevention approach will change the community norm, not just concerning community violence but also domestic violence, child abuse, youth violence, elder abuse, and random violence.

Among the many public health efforts to address the epidemic, the Los Angeles County response is typical of the approach taken by many governmental and private partnerships developed to create a comprehensive effort. In Los Angeles, a Violence Prevention Coalition was formed by the Los Angeles County Department of Health Services in 1991 in response to the public health crisis brought about by the escalating epidemic of violence. This group consists of more than 400 members who are experts in a particular category of violence or violence prevention. Coalition members include representatives from the community, business, medicine, public health, law enforcement, community-based organizations, the academic community, schools, the faith community, as well as the State of California Department of Health Services. All work together in a collaborative effort to reduce violence by measuring the magnitude of the problem, and by developing and promoting effective programs to prevent the injuries caused by violence.

The Coalition was brought together by a mutual belief that the current level of violence and the resulting injuries are unacceptable. Violence can no longer be treated as merely a law enforcement issue but must be addressed as an epidemic affecting every citizen. The Coalition members are in agreement that violence and violence prevention are the concern and responsibility of all segments of the public and private sectors. Moreover, a multi-disciplinary approach using the specific talents and expertise of the various disciplines can call attention to the problem, promote and implement prevention and intervention programs, and evaluate program effectiveness in order to significantly reduce violence and the resultant injuries. In addition, the Coalition provides a forum for influencing public policy regarding public health violence prevention in Los Angeles.

Activities of the Coalition include tracking and sponsoring legislation, investigating the media's role in violence, and advocating for a balanced approach to violence and alternatives to violence in the entertainment and journalistic media. The Coalition also identifies curricula being used by schools, studies the effect of violence on the schools, establishes a comprehensive educational campaign about the effect of violence on the community, explores community resources and programs, and develops interactions between community based organizations. Furthermore, the Coalition is exploring sources of data to quantify the scale of the problem, and drawing up standard definitions and developing linkages between data sets. A resource directory has been compiled, listing all of the resources available in Los Angeles and potential funding sources. The eclectic nature of the Coalition has encouraged the use of public health methods to evaluate the curricula being used by the schools. A series of youth fora are held, bi-monthly, with local youth to obtain their input into the process, and their suggestions for programs and solutions. Training workshops are presented to provide training to the schools. A speakers bureau has been established and the Coalition has facilitated the formation of smaller community coalitions.

Ongoing violence in Los Angeles, including the 1992 Civil Unrest, the high profile murder of the wife of a celebrity, and the subsequent disclosure of a typical domestic violence scenario have shed extended attention on the violence in Los Angeles. During the 1992 Civil Unrest, the violent rage expressed through violence on the streets resulted in more than 2,000 visits to emergency departments. During the three day period of unrest, both victims and perpetrators of street violence were overwhelmingly likely to be ethnic minority males, 15 to 34 years of age. As in the case of homicides and suicides in Los Angeles, most of the injuries in the civil unrest were due to firearms. The epidemic of violence is far from spent and the public health approach of the Coalition has never been more urgently needed.

Although the public health approach is a long term approach, it shows the greatest promise for reversing the tide of violence in homes, schools and communities. The shift in the perception of tobacco use as normal social behaviour occurred over a period of more than 20 years. Violence as a public health issue has received community attention over the past seven to ten years. It is possible to shift the social paradigm and that is the goal of the public health approach over the next decade. The entire community must be engaged in this effort to promote alternatives to violence, reduce the availability and accessibility of firearms, and to change community norms so that violence is not considered acceptable behaviour.

Bibliography

Baker, S.P., O'Neill, B., Ginsburg M.J. and Li, G. (1992), *The Injury Fact Book*, Second Edition, Oxford University Press, New York, Oxford.

Chang, A., Weiss B.P., Yuan, C. and Odeluga, M.W. (1992), *Child and adolescent injury mortality in Los Angeles County: differential mortality rates and trends: 1980-1989*, Unpublished report, Los Angeles, California.

Federal Bureau of Investigation (1993), *Crime in the United States, Uniform Crime Report, 1992*, U.S., Department of Justice, Washington DC.

Fingerhut, L. (1994), National Center for Health Statistics, Unpublished data from National Vital Statistics System.

Fingerhut, L.A. and Kleinman, J.C. (1989), *Firearm and Non-Firearm Homicide Among Teenagers: Metropolitan Status, United States 1979-1988*, Division of Analysis, National Center for Health Statistics, Center for Disease Control, Washington, DC.

Garcetti, G. (1992), *Gangs, Crime and Violence in Los Angeles County: Findings and Proposals from the District Attorney's Office*, Los Angeles County District Attorney, Los Angeles, California.

Genelin, M. (1992), *Gangs, Crime and Violence in Los Angeles County: Findings and Proposals from the District Attorney's Office*, Los Angeles County District Attorney, Los Angeles, California.

Gustafson, L., Weiss, B. and Jackson, B. (1992), *Gang Related Homicides and Assaults in Los Angeles*, presented at the American Public Health Association Meeting, November 11, Washington D.C.

Jackson, R. (1992), LAPD, unpublished data, Los Angeles.

Kellerman, A.L., Rivara, F.P., Rushforth, N.B., et al. (1993), 'Gun ownership as a risk factor for homicide in the home', *New England Journal of Medicine*, October 7, Vol. 329, No. 15, pp. 1084-91.

Los Angeles County Department of Health Services, Injury and Violence Prevention Program (1992), *Injury Mortality, A Baseline Report, 1980-1989*, Los Angeles, California.

Maxson, C. and Kline, M. (1990), 'Street gang violence: twice as great or half as great' in Huff, C. R. (ed.), *Gangs in America*, Sage Publishers, Newbury Park, California.

McBride, W. (1993), Los Angeles County Sheriff's Department, Annual Gang Report.

Meehan, P.J. and O'Carroll, P.W. (1992), 'Gangs, drugs, and homicide in Los Angeles', *American Journal of Diseases of Children*, Vol. 146, pp. 683-7.

Rosenberg, M. and Fenley, M.A. (eds.), (1991), *Violence in America: A Public Health Approach*, Oxford University Press, New York, Oxford.

Smith, D. and Laurman, B. (1988), *Child's Play: A Study of Unintended Handgun Shootings of Children*, Center to Prevent Handgun Violence, Washington, DC.

Waller, J.A. (1985), *Injury Control: A Guide to the Causes and Prevention of Trauma*, Lexington Books, Lexington, MA.

Weiss, B. (1994), County of Los Angeles Department of Health Services, Injury and Violence Prevention Program.

Weiss, B. (1993), County of Los Angeles Department of Health Services, Injury and Violence Prevention Program, data from Los Angeles County Vital Records.

Weiss B. and Strassburg, M.A. (1992), *Misclassification of Drug-Related Gang Homicides and Assaults in Los Angeles: Implications for Prevention and Intervention Strategies*, American Public Health Association meeting, November 12, Washington, D.C.

Wintemute, G. (1994), *Ring of Fire: The Handgun Makers of Southern California*, Violence Prevention Research Program, University of California, Davis, Sacramento, California.

Los Angeles County Department of Health Services, Injury and Violence Prevention Program (1992), *Injury Mortality: A Base line Report, 1986–1990*, Los Angeles, California.

Maxson, C. and Klein, M. [illegible] [illegible] gangs [illegible] as great [illegible] in [illegible] (Eds.), [illegible] *America* [illegible] Publications.

[illegible] Los Angeles County [illegible] Department.

[illegible] and O'Connell, [illegible] Los Angeles [illegible]

Rosenberg, M. and [illegible]

[illegible]

[illegible] Washington, DC.

[illegible]

[illegible]

[illegible]

[illegible] and [illegible]

[illegible]

[illegible]

[illegible] Research [illegible] University of California.

6 Numbering the dead: Counting the casualties of war

Anthony B. Zwi

Introduction

Why establish the health burden of war? We all know that war is not good for us. Spending time and effort documenting the impact of violent political conflict may appear to relegate these complex societal problems to a simple technical problem of quantification, diverting attention from necessary debate regarding the origins and solutions to these disasters.

Appreciating the burden, establishing the causes and associated risk factors, identifying vulnerable populations and potential interventions, and evaluating the cost-effectiveness of such interventions may, however, be valuable. Such scientific endeavour may assist in improving our response to these events, informing the public in countries affected by such conflicts, legitimizing public health advocacy around the promotion of peace, and attracting international funding and support for research and the development of appropriate interventions.

This paper seeks to shed light on current trends in the epidemiology of violent political conflict and its direct and indirect impact on health, to consider the influences upon such data, and to draw attention to their value and limitations.

Trends in violent political conflict

For the last 400 years each successive century has registered a progressive increase in the number of wars and associated deaths; this has greatly outstripped the increase in population over that period (Sivard, 1991). Over

107 million people have died in wars this century alone (Sivard, 1991): where earlier in the century, 90 per cent of all casualties were military; now, towards the millennium, 90 per cent are civilian (United Nations Development Programme, 1994). Prior to the ending of the Cold War, the vast majority of these violent political conflicts and wars took place in low income countries; notable exceptions were conflicts in Hungary (1956), and on the Soviet-Chinese border (1969). Many of the wars taking place in low and middle income countries had been significantly influenced by the struggle between the superpowers for military, economic and political supremacy.

The end of the Cold War seemed to promise a 'new world order', rather than the 'new world (dis)order' now commonly recognised. In the aftermath of the Cold War some conflicts, such as that in Mozambique, declined in the absence of superpower involvement, others have emerged or festered as patterns of political, economic and military support for the participants have been reviewed by their sponsors. Conflicts have also emerged with immense destructive power in the former Yugoslavia and the former Soviet Union as the demise of the latter has led to contestation for power and control at sub-national levels.

Current conflicts are largely wars within states: of the eighty-two armed conflicts between 1989 and 1992 only three were between states (United Nations Development Programme, 1994). Although frequently presented as ethnic conflicts, many of these had, and continue to have, important economic and political causes, sometimes cutting across, at other times running alongside, ethnic divisions. Such conflicts are often particularly protracted: more than half the conflicts in 1993 had been underway for a decade or more (United Nations Development Programme, 1994).

From the end of the Cold War to 1993, ninety armed conflicts[1] took place, in sixty-one locations around the world, involving at least sixty governments. About one third of the member states of the United Nations were affected. In 1995 conflicts were ongoing in Europe: Bosnia-Herzegovina, Chechnya, Croatia, Georgia and Russia; Asia: Afghanistan, Cambodia, India, Burma/Myanmar, Papua New Guinea, Philippines, Sri Lanka, Tadzhikistan; the Middle East: Israel and the Occupied Palestinian Territories, Egypt, Iran, Iraq, Turkey and Yemen; in Africa: Algeria, Angola, Burundi, Chad, Djibouti, Liberia, Mali, Niger, Rwanda, Sierra Leone, Somalia, Somaliland, Sudan and Uganda; and in the Americas: Colombia, Guatemala, Mexico and Peru (Wallensteen et al., 1995). In a number of these countries, more than one conflict was simultaneously underway, for example in both the Punjab and Kashmir in India.

While the number of conflicts has been declining in Africa and the Americas, they remain relatively stable in the Middle East and Asia, and have increased in Europe (Wallensteen et al., 1995). There has been a concomitant increase in complex political disasters in which the capacity to sustain livelihoods and life is threatened primarily by political factors and, in particular, by high levels of violence (Macrae et al., 1995b); Rwanda, Liberia, Somalia, Kurdistan and Bosnia are examples.

Factors promoting conflict include an absolute and relative lack of economic, development and environmental resources (Homer-Dixon et al., 1993), and the inequitable distribution of national resources. Additional factors may increase the propensity to violence such as high degrees of national debt and the imposition of structural adjustment and other macroeconomic reform packages by the International Monetary Fund and the World Bank. Violent conflict is an expression of economic, social, political and environmental stress.

However, seeing all wars as necessarily negative is unhelpful; there are occasions when such conflicts yield desirable social change, such as the anti-colonial struggles, or where they are necessary for protecting the victims of inequitable social and political processes. In all wars, however, both the short and medium term social and economic costs for the conflict-affected populations are considerable.

It is notable that war entails a

> ... deliberate, conscious attempt by armed parties to subdue or inflict harm on the individual members of an opposed group, to dominate or shatter the social structure of their enemy, and/or to capture, damage or destroy their enemy's material resources' (Meyers, 1991).

This highlights the fact that material damage and inflicting harm is not just a by-product of war, but is invariably its objective. An editorial in the New York Times made similar observations in the aftermath of the Gulf War:

> the bulk of the damage found was not accidental or 'collateral', but the intended consequence of the successful air campaign to destroy Iraq's war machine by attacking its industrial base and urban infrastructure. The findings raise questions about how much of that bombing was needed or justified (Frank, 1992).

A variety of typologies have been suggested for describing violent political conflict but none is ideal. Dividing violent political conflicts into structural (the inequitable distribution of social, economic and political power), repressive (the use of force by the state to undermine opposition), reactive (violent response of repressed groups in an attempt to win their political objectives), and combative (political conflicts between states or within states as a result of militarisation and miltarism) (Zwi and Ugalde, 1989) provides little insight into the causes and antecedents of such conflicts. Describing

101

conflicts as being related to either anticolonial struggles, or superpower rivalry, or the quest for regional hegemony by a nationalist group, or to conflict between classes, religions, ethnic groups and tribes, or as an attempt to access political power and economic resources, or to resolve border disputes between nations, or as ethno-nationalist struggles, masks the linkages between these different manifestations of violence.

Health effects

The extent, form, intensity, and severity of violence and its effects varies in relation to the nature of the conflict. Features of disasters, including violent political conflict, such as the scope of the impact (number of people affected, geographic extent), speed of onset (sudden, gradual, chronic), duration and social preparedness may all impact upon the effects observed (Kloos, 1992).

Both direct and indirect health effects may occur; these may present immediately, over the short, medium or long term. Within a given country there is also considerable variation in the same conflict, over time, between different areas, and in who suffers most.

Assessment of the direct casualties and deaths in both combatants and non-combatants is contentious and plagued by a lack of data, inexplicit assumptions, and the great potential for political manipulation. Measurement of indirect effects, often more significant in terms of loss of life, morbidity, disability, quality of life, burden on health services, and costs, are even more difficult and contentious to estimate.

Decisions as to what and who to include or exclude in assessments of conflict-related health burdens are subjective and greatly influence the magnitude of implied morbidity and mortality. The period over which estimates are made, the sources of information, the focus on the military and/or civilians, and whether all casualties or only those presenting to services are enumerated, will have a major effect on estimates. Real differences will also emerge as a result of the proportion of combatants within the population, the age and gender distribution in society, the nature of the conflict, the degree of access to services and emergency care, and the nature of the destructive technologies employed.

Direct health effects

A review of current knowledge of war-related mortality and morbidity among military forces (Garfield et al., 1991) shows that even for those who are actively involved in conducting such wars, the data are unreliable, inaccurate and imprecise and are affected by real and artefactual factors (Table 6.1).

This is so despite the fact that the military may have control over its own personnel, including their location and their care, and suggests that efforts should be made to standardize, or at the very least, make explicit the basis of estimates from different battlefields and forces.

Table 6.1
Influences on assessment of direct injuries and deaths amongst military forces
(examples of possible influences)

Nature of the conflict	Inter-state or intra-state Conventional war vs. 'low intensity' conflict
Personnel involved	Proportion of troops exposed to combat Type of force involved: logistic, infantry, land, sea or air-based Age, sex, prior health status of combatants
Weapons, protective clothing and transport systems available	Technology: machetes, firearms, landmines, bombs 'protective clothing': heavy boots, helmets, flak-jackets Transport systems: armoured troop carriers, tanks, helicopters
Medical care	Prior to combat: prophylaxis against prevalent diseases, immunization During combat: availability of emergency services, life support, and evacuation facilities Post-trauma: physical and psychological rehabilitation and support services
Recording systems	Whose injuries are recorded? Variability in definitions such as 'killed in action', 'died of wounds', 'wounded in action' Variation in denominators used Whether and how indirect effects enumerated Availability of comparative and trend data

Source: adapted from Garfield and Neugat, 1991

No attempt will be made here to survey the extent of health damage which has occurred in recent conflicts. However, it is clear that the impact on health can be extensive. In Mozambique for example, the anti-government force Renamo killed 100,000 civilians in 1986 and 1987 alone, and over four million people (nearly a third of the population) were displaced.

Table 6.2 describes the range and variety of direct war-related health problems, in terms of morbidity, mortality and disability. An attempt to quantify the impact of over thirty years of war in Ethiopia suggested that approximately one million people died, about half of whom were civilians (Kloos, 1992). About one third of the 300,000 soldiers returning from the front after the end of the conflict had been injured or disabled. By 1984, well before the end of the war in 1991, over 40,000 people had lost one or more limbs in the conflict (Kloos, 1992).

Table 6.2
Quantifying direct effects of violent political conflict
(examples of the range of possible effects)

Mortality	Injuries and associated fatalities
	Preventable diseases: measles, diphtheria, polio, tetanus
	Deaths preventable by medical care: asthma, diabetes, emergency surgery
Morbidity	Injuries: landmines, burns, poisoning
	Violence against women: rape and domestic violence
	Water-related diseases: cholera, typhoid, diarrhoea
	Vector-borne diseases: malaria, helminthiasis, onchocerciasis, typhus, trypanosomiasis
	Other communicable diseases: tuberculosis, acute respiratory infections, HIV/AIDS and sexually transmitted diseases
	Reproductive health: increased levels of prematurity, low-birth weight and stillbirths
	Nutritional deficiency disorders
	Mental health: anxiety, depression, post-traumatic stress disorder
	Genetic: long-term effects associated with exposure to radiation and chemical and biological agents
Disability	Physical and psychological

A number of health problems may be greatly exacerbated in wartime. Infant mortality may rise in association with reduced access to health and immunization services, impairment of the basic infrastructure necessary to promote health, poorer nutrition for children and their mothers, and population displacement. Preventable diseases such as measles, tetanus and diphtheria may become epidemic. During the Ugandan civil war the infant mortality rate rose to above 600 per 1000 in certain war-affected areas (Dodge, 1990). UNICEF has reported that declines in infant mortality occured in all countries in Southern Africa over the period 1960-1986, with the exception of Mozambique and Angola which were the two countries most affected by vicious civil wars in this period (UNICEF, 1989).

In Zepa (former Yugoslavia), a UN-controlled 'safe-haven' which was subsequently overrun by the Bosnian Serbs, perinatal and childhood mortality rates doubled after only one year of war. In Sarajevo, deliveries of premature babies had doubled and average birthweights fallen by 20 per cent by 1993, two years into the war. In Bosnia, fewer than 35 per cent of children were being immunized, compared with 95 per cent before the war (Mann et al., 1994; Horton, 1994).

The occurrence and transmission of a variety of communicable diseases is increased due to such factors as the decline in immunization coverage, population movements, and the lack of access to health services. A war-related measles epidemic in Nicaragua was attributed in large part to the declining ability of the health service to immunize those at risk in conflict-affected areas (Garfield et al., 1987). The decline in malaria control activities was associated with epidemics in Ethiopia (Kloos, 1992), Nicaragua (Garfield et al., 1987) and Mozambique (Cliff et al., 1988) highlighting the vulnerability of complex disease control programmes in periods of conflict. The increased rates of malaria in war-affected populations are attributed to troop movements, the inability to carry out timely disease control activities, and shortages of the health personnel needed to conduct control programmes in peripheral areas (Garfield et al., 1987, p.616). In Ethiopia, epidemics of louse-borne typhus and relapsing fever were associated with crowded army camps, prisons, and relief camps, as well as the sale of infected blankets and clothes to local communities by retreating soldiers (Kloos, 1992). In Rwanda, epidemics of water-related disease (shigella dysentery and cholera) led to the death, within a month, of 6-10 per cent of the refugee population arriving in Zaire (Goma Epidemiology Group, 1995). The crude death rate of 20-35 per 10,000 population per day was two to three times higher than that in previously reported refugee populations (Goma Epidemiology Group, 1995).

'High risk situations' for HIV transmission may also occur in times of conflict and their aftermath (Zwi and Ugalde, 1991; Smallman-Raynor et al.,

1991; Kloos, 1992). HIV infection has reached high levels in many armed forces; the ability of these men to command sexual services from local women, through payment or force, the movement of troops to different parts of the country, and their ultimate return to divergent regions of the country after demobilization, present significant risks to women. Peace-keeping forces may pose risks for sexually transmitted diseases and HIV through stimulating a local commercial sex market, drawing women into prostitution.

Nutrition programmes and community-based programmes, such as the provision of post-partum care, may be severely constrained by political conflict (Garfield et al., 1987); outreach services, as well as those which are hospital-based, may decline as a result of services being put out of commission, absent health service staff, and population movement.

Refugees and internally displaced populations, most fleeing from the effects of conflict (United Nations High Commissioner for Refugees, 1993), or the direct effect of 'ethnic cleansing', have raised mortality rates, often resulting from the combined effects of poor nutrition, increased vulnerability to communicable diseases, diminished access to health services, poor environmental conditions, anxiety and stress. A study of the impact of the war in Bosnia drew attention to the creation of new 'vulnerable' populations such as those in isolated enclaves or forced to flee as a result of 'ethnic cleansing' (Russbach et al., 1994). Recent reviews of the health of refugees and displaced populations have revealed massively raised mortality, at its worst up to sixty times the expected death rates during the acute phase of displacement (Toole et al., 1990; Toole et al., 1993; Center for Disease Control, 1992). In Monrovia, Liberia, the death rate among civilians displaced in 1990 during the civil war was seven times higher than the pre-war death rate (MSF, Holland, quoted in Center for Disease Control, 1992).

Data are scant on levels of war-related disability, although they are obviously high from what little we know. A nation-wide disability survey conducted in 1982 after the liberation struggle in Zimbabwe revealed that 13 per cent of all physical disabilities were the direct result of the war. Estimates of landmine-related amputations and disabilities are sobering: 36,000 in Cambodia (6,000 in 1990 alone; i.e. one in every 236 Cambodians has lost at least one limb after detonating a mine), 20,000 in Angola, 8,000 in Mozambique, 15,000 in Uganda, and unknown numbers in Afghanistan. In former Yugoslavia, over 3 million mines have been laid, and 50,000 per week continued to be sown, without any markers or maps, in late 1994 (O'Brien, 1994). Over 30 million mines were laid in Afghanistan in the 1980s.

The costs of are both medical and social (Stover et al., 1994; Kakar, 1995). In Hargeisa Hospital, Somaliland, 74.6 per cent of the landmine-related injuries treated from February 1991 to February 1992 were in children between the ages of five and fifteen years (Physicians for Human Rights (USA), 1992). Children may inadvertently play with mines, mine detonators and grenades, resulting in amputations, injuries to the eyes, and blindness. There are also anecdotal reports of people using landmines as a means of protecting their own personal security, around the perimeter fence of their property, for example.

The cost of total clearance is enormous (estimated at $30-$85 billion worldwide [O'Brien, 1994]) and therefore unaffordable: this means that many mines will be left intact, large tracts of land left unusable, and death and limb loss likely to continue for decades. Even where mines are actively being removed, it has been estimated that one person would die and two would be injured for every 5,000 mines inactivated.

The mental health impact is influenced by a range of factors including the nature of the conflict, the form of trauma experienced (including that directly inflicted, as in the case of torture and other repressive violence), the individual and community response to these pressures, the cultural context in which they occur, and the psychological health of those affected prior to the event. The mental health impacts resulting from conflict have been well reviewed (Summerfield, 1991; De Girolamo, 1993).

Psychological stresses are also associated with displacement, both forced and voluntary, and result from loss and grief, social isolation, loss of status, loss of community and, in some settings, acculturation to new environments (Quirk et al., 1994). Manifestations of such stress include depression and anxiety, psychosomatic ailments, intra-familial conflict, alcohol abuse and antisocial behaviour (Summerfield, 1991). Single and isolated refugees, as well as women who are single-handedly managing a family, may be at particular risk.

Summerfield (1991) cautions against assuming that populations do not have the ability and resilience to respond to these adverse circumstances; authors in South Africa have similarly argued that not everybody exposed to massive degrees of trauma become 'victims': their ability to respond is strengthened by their participation in what is perceived to be a legitimate struggle (Gibson, 1989). The medical model which labels individuals with a particular complex of symptoms and signs as having 'post-traumatic stress syndrome' is culture-bound and may fail to take account of ongoing stressors: it cannot address the complexity of human response, including the interpretation and adaptation to the effects of violence (Summerfield, 1991). Recent work by Bracken and colleagues (1995) has reinforced these cautions, and highlights the importance of appreciating the subjective meaning of the violence or trauma, the way in which distress is experienced and reported, the type of general support available to the individual, and the type of therapies available and appropriate to the needs identified.

In the longer term, the adverse effects of children witnessing, being victims of, or participating in violent political conflict are uncertain. Children may have been forced under duress to commit such atrocities as burning down their own homes or killing a family member. How South African or Palestinian youths see the world, after engaging in violent political struggles for much of their 'childhood', and the extent to which they see violence as the only mechanism for resolving conflict and overcoming adversity will perhaps become apparent in coming decades. While most such experiences may leave little permanent effect, it is quite conceivable that amongst a minority, the effects will be substantial. For such individuals, their attitudes towards society, ability to obtain employment or to act as positive role-models for their children, to be responsible parents, and to have healthy inter-personal relationships in times of peace may all be disrupted. The long-term psychosocial effects of major political conflict and violence have yet to be adequately explored. It is increasingly clear, however, that recovery over time is intrinsically linked to the reconstruction of social and economic networks, cultural institutions and respect for human rights (Bracken et al., 1995).

Effects on health services

The impact of conflict on health services are wide-ranging and will not be discussed in any detail here (see Table 6.3). Recent studies from a variety of conflicts draw attention to their impact (Lee and Haines, 1991; Kloos, 1992; Mann et al., 1994; Hall and Carney, 1995; Goma Epidemiology Group, 1995).

Attempts to quantify the impact on health services of the US-led coalition against Iraq in 1991 revealed the damage to the Iraqi health system which before the war was accessible to 90 per cent of the population and able to immunize the vast majority of children under the age of five years. By the end of the war, many hospitals and clinics had been severely damaged or closed; those still operating in the months after the war were forced to cope with much larger catchment populations, rendering them unable to provide appropriate care (Lee and Haines, 1991). Damage to infrastructure, including water supplies, electricity and sewage disposal, exacerbated both the determinants of ill health and the operation of health services.

Table 6.3
Impact of violent political conflict on health services

Access to services	Greater difficulty due to curfews, anti-personnel mines, etc.
	Avoidance of services for fear of being identified as participant in conflict
Service infrastructure	Destruction of clinics
	Disruption of referral systems
	Destruction of health service roads and vehicles
	Destruction of lines of communication from periphery to centre and between peripheral services
Human resources	Injury, killing, kidnapping of health workers
	Poor morale of health workers
	Displaced and/or exiled health workers
	Difficulty attracting health workers to peripheral areas
	Disruption of training and supervisory activities
Equipment and supplies	Lack of drugs
	Lack of maintenance
	Poor access to new technologies
	Inability to maintain cold chain for vaccines
Impact on health service activity	Shift from primary to tertiary level care
	Increased urbanization of provision
	Overburdening of health services with caring for wounded rather than community health activities
	Impaired monitoring of pregnant women and those with young children
	Disrupted surveillance and health information systems
	Disrupted infectious disease control programmes eg. malaria spraying, public health campaigns, case-finding, partner notification
	Outreach activities disrupted by lack of transport, mining of roads, destroyed peripheral centres, etc.
	Tendency towards aid dependency and increased donor influence
	Tendency towards centralized vertical programmes

Table 6.3 continued

Impact on health   Undermined national capacity
policy formulation   Inability to control and co-ordinate activities of non-
       governmental organizations and donor organisations
       Limited information systems upon which to base
       policy
       Limited international debate and consultation
       Impaired community structures and participation in
       local government
       Limited participation in international health debates

Relief activities   Limited access to many areas
       Increased expense in delivering food and other relief
       supplies
       Tendency to high degree of verticality
       Danger to relief personnel
       Impaired co-ordination and communication between
       agencies

Sources: Zwi and Ugalde, 1989; Zwi and Ugalde, 1991; Dodge, 1990; Garfield et al., 1992; Garfield, 1989; Macrae et al., 1995a; Macrae et al., 1995b

Poorer supply of drugs has been associated with increases in medically preventable causes of death such as asthma, diabetes and many infectious diseases. The quality of available care may deteriorate greatly; reports from Northern Somalia indicate that amputations had been performed without intravenous antibiotics, leading to high rates of infection (Physicians for Human Rights (USA), 1992); more recent data have similarly emerged from the former Yugoslavia.

Human resources are seriously affected by conflict. In Uganda, half the doctors and 80 per cent of the pharmacists left the country in search of more rewarding opportunities between 1972 and 1985. In Mozambique, the country was left with only 15 per cent of the 550 doctors present in the country before independence (Walt et al., 1986).

Indirect effects

Conflict may also indirectly have an impact on health, through its influence on infrastructure and the determinants of health (Table 6.4). Water and sanitation, for example, are often seriously disrupted by war and conflict. In both southern Sudan and Uganda, even ordinary hand pumps in villages were specifically destroyed by government troops in rebel-held areas, and by guerrillas in government-held areas (Dodge, 1990). In the conflict between the US-led coalition and Iraq, water supplies, sewage removal and other sanitation services were drastically affected by saturation bombing. After the conflict, it was estimated that 2.5 million people, one eighth of the Iraqi population, were no longer able to obtain water from the government system; even when available it was of doubtful quality. The availability of drinkable water declined dramatically from 7 million cubic meters/day to only 1.5 million cubic meters/day; a shortage of sulphate and chlorine, necessary for water purification, was experienced and electrical power, required for water purification and sewage removal, was down to 4 per cent of the pre-war level (Aga Khan, 1991). In addition, bacteriological testing was unreliable and haphazard; cases of typhoid, cholera and gastro-enteritis surged.

The impact of conflict on community participation may be positive or negative. In some countries, there is evidence of conflict enhancing community mobilization, participation and control over local decision-making. Experiences in Nicaragua (Frieden et al., 1987), Mozambique (Walt et al., 1986), Vietnam, Eritrea (Sabo et al., 1989) and Tigray (Barnabas, 1995) suggest that conflict may present an important opportunity for community mobilization and organization and that communities may come together to respond to external threats. A key challenge is to maintain such supportive structures in the aftermath of conflict.

In many other struggles, particularly those of the 'low intensity' form, such as those in Nicaragua and Mozambique, there is evidence of community leaders and social structures being particularly targeted for assassination. The struggle between Sendero Luminosa and the Peruvian government demonstrates how destructive such struggles can be. The immediate and longer term effect of such action is difficult to quantify: the disruption of local systems of democracy and accountability and the negative effects of discouraging involvement in community affairs may be profound and long-lasting.

There is also good evidence of the specific targeting of food production and distribution activities during periods of conflict (Table 6.5). Food production was directly disrupted in Ethiopia through preventing farmers from planting and harvesting their crops and by the looting of seeds and livestock by soldiers (Kloos, 1992). In Tigray, the conscription of men, the mining of land, the confiscation of food, and the slaughter of cattle were widespread (Kloos, 1992, p. 349). The loss of livestock deprives farmers of an asset needed to put land into production; it therefore has an adverse effect both immediately and in the future. In Eritrea, about 40 per cent of the land area was not cultivable due to similar disruption of activities and access to land (Kloos, 1992, p. 350). In Bosnia, the Bosnian Serbs specifically sought to control the inflow of relief supplies into besieged cities such as Sarajevo.

Table 6.4
Indirect influence of violent political conflict on health and development

Infrastructure damage	Damage to water supplies, sanitation, sewage disposal Disruption of electrical power Destruction of bridges, roads, railways, airports and transport systems Communication system dysfunction
Health and welfare	Direct and indirect impact on services (see Tables 6.2 and 6.3)
Disrupted human settlements	People forced to flee their land and homes as refugees and internally displaced Increased levels of urbanisation Forced resettlement
Environmental	Health impact of environmental damage Direct environmental destruction Destruction and contamination of areas previously available for agriculture Reduced availability of wood-fuel and other local resources Disrupted food security (see Table 6.5)
Impact on social organisation	Impact (positive or negative) on community participation Direct targeting of community leaders and representatives Reduced climate for accountable local government Human rights abuses

Table 6.4 continued

Macroeconomic	Diversion of budgets away from social sector in favour of military expenditure
	Post-conflict expenditure on reconstruction
	Reduced availability and increase in prices of food and other goods due to scarcity and market manipulation
	Loss of external markets, high costs of imports
	Loss of tourism
	General disruption of trade and migration activities
	Increased prices of basic materials

Forced population resettlement, used by a number of governments for security and ideological reasons, may also have severe adverse impacts upon health. In the two to three years after 1985, more than 5.7 million people, 15.4 per cent of the total rural population, had been moved to villages as part of an enforced Ethiopian government programme (Hodes et al., 1988).

The economic impact of conflict may be profound (Stewart, 1993). In Ethiopia, military expenditure increased from 11.2 per cent of the government budget in 1974-75 to 36.5 per cent by 1990-91, the health budget declined from 6.1 per cent in 1973-74 to 3.5 per cent in 1985/86 and 3.2 per cent in 1990-91 (Kloos, 1992). Similar trends occurred in Nicaragua (Garfield et al., 1992). There are also significant effects on productivity and exports, reductions in the ability to collect tax revenue, loss of human capital, loss of tourism and other usual sources of income, and great scope for price manipulation, speculation and profit-making, often at the expense of the majority of the population.

In the post-conflict period, the costs of reconstruction may be staggering. It has been estimated, for example, that Iraq will require $110-$200 billion and Kuwait $60-$95 billion to repair the war damage from the US-led coalition vs. Iraq war (Lee et al., 1991). In contrast, the goals adopted by the World Summit for Children in 1991 required $20 billion for their global implementation.

This begs a bigger question addressed elsewhere: whether health systems should be simply rehabilitated and reconstructed in their pre-war image, or whether opportunities should be taken to redefine the health care system (Macrae et al., 1995a; Macrae et al., 1995b).

Problems of gathering and using relevant data

The discussion above has highlighted the form which the damage to health and health systems may take. In most situations, the data required to assess all these forms of destruction, both immediate and in the longer term, direct and indirect, are sorely lacking, and often not wanted by some of the parties involved. A UN spokesman in Angola argued that only general estimates of war-related deaths was possible. He said 'You simply cannot count bodies in any war. There are other priorities' (Black, 1993).

Rapid assessment methods may, however, be used to shed light on war damage and are increasingly being used (Toole, 1994).

Table 6.5
Mechanisms compromising food security during periods of violent political conflict

Disruption and destruction	Direct destruction of food stores
	Looting of seeds, cattle, equipment and food stores
	Direct targeting of relief activities
	Disruption of coping strategies such as denying access to areas of wild-food availability and denying family members opportunity to migrate
	Disrupted cattle-grazing patterns
	Attacks on and restriction of access to markets
	Manipulating prices of food commodities
	Enforced changes to farming systems
	Preventing access to land through planting landmines
	Laying siege to cities (Sarajevo, Juba, etc.) and towns
Selective provision of food	Providing food only in areas where political support is provided or desired
	Diversion of food aid to military forces
Population relocation	Moving populations away from their lands
	Forcing scattered rural populations into villages for easier control

Sources: Macrae and Zwi, 1994a ; Kloos, 1992

Data collection, collation, analysis, interpretation and dissemination may all be affected by ongoing conflict.

A number of methodologic challenges for wartime epidemiology have been specified (Armenian, 1989; Armenian, 1986; Chen et al., 1994): wars are dynamic situations, constantly changing with periodic exacerbations and remissions, thus requiring a degree of continuous monitoring and surveillance; the normal public health and information systems are paralysed implying that innovative approaches need to be developed to gather information; the serious lack of trained personnel may make the research team dependent on voluntary workers requiring intensive support and supervision; compromises in scientific rigour may be necessary in order to ensure that at least some data are collected, for example from a limited number of sentinel surveillance sites; there may be security and personal sensitivities about revealing the circumstances of injury and death occurrences during wartime. Researchers may themselves face threats to their personal security, particularly if they come to be associated with one or other parties to the conflict.

The disruption in routine data collection means that we are often left with 'guesstimates' with data reliability, validity and completeness open to dispute. The denominators for morbidity and mortality are often unknown. The displacement or exodus of large numbers of people, during times of conflict, makes it extremely difficult to estimate population denominator data, a crucial element in determining rates of disease or mortality.

Despite these difficulties, a variety of practical measures have been used in relatively controlled environments to measure mortality in refugee camps and among displaced populations: these include data gathered from hospital and burial records, from burial site surveillance, and from verbal autopsies, a method devised to determine the cause of death by interviewing family members about the history, signs and symptoms experienced prior to death (Center for Disease Control, 1992; Moore et al., 1993). Problems related to recall bias, failure to report perinatal deaths, inaccurate denominators, lack of standardized reporting procedures all compound the problems of data collection. Yet, gathering such data in refugee settings may be substantially more feasible than in other situations of conflict, including those of internally displaced populations, where communities are widely dispersed, services virtually non-existent, personnel training and supervision extremely difficult, and infrastructure for the collation and analysis of data are poor or nonexistent. Data collected in these settings may nevertheless demonstrate the threat to health in these contexts: in Somalia, 74 per cent of a group of displaced children under five died between April and November 1992 (Moore et al., 1993), far above the mortality rate which would have been experienced in the absence of conflict even in such an impoverished and under-served nation.

Recent experience of using rapid assessment methods have demonstrated how best to utilise available data (Toole, 1994). Information needs to be collected by multidisciplinary teams, using both quantitative and qualitative methods. Standard epidemiological techniques, where possible, should be supplemented by other data such as interviews with key informants, record reviews and limited community surveys. Community leaders, local health facilities, non-governmental organizations and health workers all have access to useful and important information and reflect important viewpoints and insights.

The time taken to perform rapid assessments will depend on the remoteness of the location, security, ease of access, degree of cooperation of local authorities, number of agencies operating, communication and logistics. Rapid assessments should include the establishment of an ongoing public health monitoring and surveillance system, focusing on mortality, morbidity, nutritional status, and diseases with epidemic potential (Toole, 1994). Efforts should be made to construct systems which can be maintained in the aftermath of the war.

Data may be improved by standardizing approach, techniques and definitions. Standardising the coding of war-related morbidity and mortality may support longer term advocacy. The ICD coding system only lists direct war-related deaths, primarily in the form of direct injuries. Indirect effects, such as the deaths of children from disrupted immunization systems, or from water-related diseases after the destruction of water and sanitation supplies, would not be recorded as having any war-related basis. Future ICD systems would benefit from an additional code being allocated to a death which occurs in a conflict period or conflict zone: this would provide a more accurate indication of the health-related burden of this problem. However, the political nature of such statistics would still ensure that the precise burden is rarely described.

Additional difficulties may be related to determining the 'conflict share' or population attributable fraction associated with a variety of manifestations of ill health in populations. Other ongoing phenomena also detrimental to health, such as economic crisis and gross inequalities in society, may simultaneously be present: disentangling their effect from that of the violent political conflict would not be a worthwhile exercise as they are, in any case, related to one another. It might be more sensible to consider them together as a 'maldevelopment and conflict' cluster of factors impacting adversely upon health: in Ethiopia, the effects of war, drought, government repression and misdirected government economic policy all influenced health outcomes simultaneously (Kloos, 1992).

Making use of the data

Data on war-related health damage are highly political, probably even more so than data on other politicized health problems such as inequalities in health, interpersonal violence, cholera, HIV, or malnutrition. As a result, each party to the conflict has its own reasons for collecting and presenting figures in a particular way. This virtually guarantees that many of the data published are highly biased - in some cases to assert that fewer injuries and deaths occurred than in reality, in others to assert the opposite. Understanding where the data come from and how the estimates were derived is crucial to building an accurate picture of what has occurred. Triangulating data of different sorts, from different sources, may be required to build an accurate estimate of true experience.

Many governments may resist making such information available. Neither the Iraqi government, nor the US authorities had any interest in publishing precise details of the direct impact of the Gulf war. For Iraq, the death of over 100,000 people and injuries to 300,000 soldiers, plus the deaths of at least 7,000 civilians from coalition bombing highlighted the futility of the war. For the United States, disclosing the body-count would undermine the carefully cultivated media image of the war as a clean, highly 'targeted', 'surgical intervention', a war between machines, not men, with very little 'collateral damage' (Frank, 1992). The discourse employed, such as 'circular error probability' which described civilian deaths in Vietnam, obfuscate the reality of war damage (see, for example, Pilger, 1992). The highly political nature of such data, and the unwillingness to publish available estimates and insights, was highlighted by the dismissal of a US Census Bureau demographer who made available the Bureau's working estimates of Gulf war deaths.

When Israel invaded the Lebanon in 1982, journalists on the Palestinian side reported thousands of Lebanese civilian casualties, while Israel counted only a handful of dead 'terrorists' (Black, 1993). In civil wars, the truth often remains elusive. The winners write the history of the conflict 'through the prism of their own prejudice and propaganda' (Black, 1993).

Despite these difficulties, some sources of data are available and should be used. The Center for Disease Control (1992) indicate the role and function of a health information system in times of emergencies: to follow trends in health status, establish health care priorities, detect and respond to epidemics, evaluate programme effectiveness and service coverage, ensure efficient use of resources targeted to areas in greatest need, and to evaluate the quality of care delivered.

Comparison of pre-war with intra-war and post-war data may be of value. So too may be comparing health status and health determinants with neighbouring countries with similar Gross National Product per capita. As mentioned earlier, however, attributing specific changes in health status to violent political conflict probably needs to recognise that it is not only conflict but a related set of conditions such as maldevelopment, inequalities and economic crisis which have led to health declines.

Sources of information on the effects of conflict may include records of health services still operating (public, private-for-profit, non-governmental - both indigenous and foreign), key informants such as local government officials, health workers, women and community leaders. Both qualitative and quantitative information should be sought - all will help put together a picture of what is happening at the local level. Data based on case studies and small numbers need cautious interpretation, especially in terms of generalisability beyond the study setting itself.

Table 6.6
Factors influencing the availability of data on the health effects of violent political conflict

Real difficulties	Denominators unknown Disrupted record-keeping and reporting systems Overloaded services (coroners, funeral parlours, public health services)
Biases	Governments have little incentive for true effects to be publicised Parties to the conflict may select data that supports their political case Media may present most dramatic figures without assessing their validity

Data collated at a global level include those estimates of the Stockholm International Peace Research Institute and Sivard's regular Review of Military and Social Expenditures. These documents provide a carefully researched, albeit conservative (Milton Leitenberg, personal communication, 1995), estimate regarding conflict-related human destruction. National governments, multilateral organizations, non-government organizations and the media may collate data about the human costs of war; these however, may be distorted by the sources from which they are derived and may suffer from incompleteness and the other problems of validity and accuracy referred to above. Additional sources include international press and United Nations reports: these tend to draw upon estimates collated and/or reported by national governments, international organizations, press and journalists, and non-governmental services operating in the conflict-affected area.

Conclusion

War and other forms of violent political conflict are detrimental to health. Improving our understanding of how detrimental it is, what form this takes, what can be done to mitigate its effects during and after conflict, are important. Improving methods of identifying those situations which are vulnerable to conflict and instituting early primary prevention interventions may help avoid organized violence (Gellert, 1995; Zwi, 1995).

Data may be useful in shifting policy decisions, through their impact on decision-makers, either directly or through the media. Figures, however, can be manipulated by those on all sides: this calls for a high index of suspicion in accepting data supplied by a participant to the conflict. In any case, we must recognize that the counts, numbers, and data are just one of many influences which may be influential in generating a media, public and/or policy-maker response.

Requiring governments to record and make public data is an important intervention necessary for the promotion of transparency and accountability; but such action would need to be carefully monitored if the propensity to manipulate such figures is to be controlled.

Experience of innovative approaches to operating public health systems during periods of conflict should be documented. It would also be beneficial to begin to describe and further develop mechanisms for maintaining support to peripheral health workers and public health and management activities if some of the adverse effects of conflict on health are to be addressed during these tumultuous periods. Even more important is identifying early warning systems for public health disasters, a greatly underdeveloped area of activity[2].

Finally, it is the civilian populations worldwide, the victims of war, and the worldwide community, that stand to gain from publicizing and auditing the effects of conflict. Health workers can play some part in ensuring that such debate takes place. Ultimately, health workers, epidemiologists and statisticians should commit themselves to placing data on the impact of conflict in the public domain. We should also work actively with others to promote the early identification of populations vulnerable to conflict, and the rapid resolution of those conflicts which are in process, if further deaths, disabilities and morbidity are to be avoided.

Note

1 Defined here as armed contested incompatabilities which concern government and/or territory, where the use of armed force by two parties, of which at least one is the government of a state, results in at least 25 battle-related deaths (Wallensteen and Axell, 1994). The precise definition used has implications for the number of countries considered to be engaged in a violent political conflict.

2 Understanding the 'post'-conflict milieu and the avenues for a redefinition of health systems in the aftermath of a conflict will continue to exercise rational govenments, the donor community and non-governmental organisations (Macrae, 1995b).

Acknowledgement

The author works within the Health Economics and Financing Programme, funded by the Overseas Development Administration (UK). The views represented here should not, however be taken to reflect those of any organisation. The author acknowledges the influence of his colleagues at the Health Policy Unit on his work in relation to conflict and health.

Bibliography

Armenian, H.K. (1986), 'In wartime: Options for epidemiology', *American Journal of Epidemiology*, Vol. 124, pp. 28-32.

Armenian, H.K. (1989), 'Perceptions from epidemiologic research in an endemic war', *Social Science and Medicine*, Vol. 28, No. 7, pp. 643-8.

Barnabas, G.A. (1995), 'Community mobilisation in Tigray', Unpublished, Addis Ababa.

Black, I. (1993), 'Why count the bodies when it's not our war?', *Guardian*, 18 September 1993, London, p. 27.

Bloom, S., Miller, J.M., Warner, J. and Winkler, P. (ed.s), (1994), *Hidden Casualties. The Environmental, Health and Political Consequences of the Persian Gulf War*, Earthscan, London.

Bracken, P.J., Giller, J.E. and Summerfield, D. (1995), 'Psychological responses to war and atrocity: the limitations of current concepts', *Social Science and Medicine*, Vol. 40, No. 8, pp. 1073-82.

Center for Disease Control (1992), 'Famine affected, refugee, and displaced populations: Recommendations for public health issues', *Morbidity and Mortality Weekly Report*, Vol. 41, pp. rr-13.

Chen, L.C. and Rietveld, A. (1994), 'Human security during complex humanitarian emergencies: rapid assessment and institutional capabilities', *Medicine and Global Survival*, Vol. 1, pp. 156-63.

Cliff, J. and Noormahomed, A.R. (1988), 'Health as a target: South Africa's destabilization of Mozambique', *Social Science and Medicine*, Vol. 27, No. 7, pp. 717-22.

De Girolamo, G. (1993), 'International perspectives on the treatment and prevention of post-traumatic stress disorder' in Wilson, J.P. and Raphael, B. (eds.), *International Handbook of Traumatic Stress Syndromes*, Plenum Press, New York and London, pp. 935-46.

Dodge, C.P. (1990), 'Health implications of war in Uganda and Sudan', *Social Science and Medicine*, Vol. 31, No. 6, pp. 691-98.

Dodge, C.P. and Wiebe, P.D. (eds.), (1985), *Crisis in Uganda: The Breakdown of Health Services*, Pergamon Press, Oxford.

Frank, A.G. (1992), 'Third World War: A political economy of the Gulf War and the new world order', *Third World Quarterly*, Vol. 13, No. 2, pp. 267-82.

Frieden, T. and Garfield, R. (1987), 'Popular participation in health in Nicaragua', *Health Policy and Planning*, Vol. 2, No. 2, pp. 162-70.

Garfield, R.M. (1989), 'War-related changes in health and health services in Nicaragua', *Social Science and Medicine*, Vol. 28, No. 7, pp. 669-76.

Garfield, R.M. and Neugat, A.I. (1991), 'Epidemiologic analysis of warfare. A historical review', *Journal of the American Medical Association*, Vol. 266, No.5, pp. 688-92.

Garfield, R. and Williams, G. (1992), *Health Care in Nicaragua*, Oxford University Press, Oxford.

Garfield, R.M., Frieden, T. and Vermund, S.H. (1987), 'Health-related outcomes of war in Nicaragua', *American Journal of Public Health*, Vol. 77, No. 5, pp. 615-8.

Gellert, G.A. (1995), 'Humanitarian responses to mass violence perpetrated against vulnerable populations', *British Medical Journal*, Vol. 311, pp. 995-1002.

Gibson, K. (1989), 'Children in political violence', *Social Science and Medicine*, Vol. 28, No. 7, pp. 659-68.

Goma Epidemiology Group (1995), 'Public health impact of Rwandan refugee crisis: what happened in Goma, Zaire, in July 1994?', *Lancet*, Vol. 345, pp. 339-44.

Hall, P. and Carney, A. (1995), 'Politics by genocide', *Medicine and War*, Vol. 11, pp. 4-17.

Hodes, R.M and Kloos, H. (1988), 'Health and medical care in Ethiopia', *New England Journal of Medicine*, Vol. 319, No. 14, pp. 918-24.

Homer-Dixon, T.F., Boutwell, J.H. and Rathjens, G.W. (1993), 'Environmental change and violent conflict', *Scientific American*, February edition, pp. 16-23.

Horton, R. (1994), '... on the brink of humanitarian disaster', *Lancet*, Vol. 343, p. 1053.

Kakar, F. (1995), *Direct and Indirect Consequences of Landmines on Public Health*, World Health Organization, Geneva.

Kloos, H. (1992), 'Health impacts of war in Ethiopia', *Disasters*, Vol. 16, pp. 347-54.

Lee, I. and Haines, A. (1991), 'Health costs of the Gulf War', *British Medical Journal*, Vol. 303, pp. 303-6.

Macrae, J. and Zwi, A. (1994a), 'Famine, complex emergencies and international policy in Africa: An overview' in Macrae, J. and Zwi, A. (eds.), *War & Hunger: Rethinking International Responses to Complex Emergencies*, Zed Books in Association with Save the Children Fund (UK), London, pp. 6-36.

Macrae, J. and Zwi, A. (eds.), (1994b), *War & Hunger: Rethinking International Responses to Complex Emergencies*, Zed Books in association with Save the Children Fund (UK), London.

Macrae, J., Zwi, A. and Birungi, H. (1995a), *A healthy peace? Rehabilitation and development of the health sector in a 'post'-conflict situation. The case of Uganda*, Public Health and Policy Report No. 14, Department of Public Health and Policy, London School of Hygiene and Tropical Medicine, London.

Macrae, J., Zwi, A. and Forsythe, V. (1995b), *Post-conflict rehabilitation: Preliminary issues for consideration by the health sector*, Public Health and Policy Report No. 16, Department of Public Health and Policy, London School of Hygiene and Tropical Medicine, London.

Mann, J., Drucker E., Tarantola, D. and McCabe, M.P. (1994), 'Bosnia: The war against public health', *Medicine and Global Survival*, Vol. 1, pp. 130-46.

Meyers, B. (1991), 'Disaster study of war', *Disasters*, Vol. 15, pp. 318-30.

Moore, P.S., Marfin, A.A., Quenemoen, L.E. et al. (1993), 'Mortality rates in displaced and resident populations of central Somalia during 1992 famine', *Lancet*, Vol. 341, pp. 935-8.

O'Brien, E. (1994), 'The land mine crisis: a growing epidemic of mutilation', *Lancet*, Vol. 344, p. 1522.

Physicians for Human Rights (USA) (1992), *Hidden Enemies. Landmines in Northern Somalia*, Physicians for Human Rights (USA), Boston.

Pilger, J. (1992), *Distant Voices*, Vintage, London.

Quirk, G.J. and Casco, L. (1994), 'Stress disorders of families of the disappeared: A controlled study in Honduras', *Social Science and Medicine*, Vol. 39, No. 12, pp. 1675-9.

Russbach, R. and Fink, D. (1994), 'Humanitarian action in current armed conflicts: Opportunities and obstacles', *Medicine and Global Survival*, Vol. 1, pp. 188-99.

Sabo, L.E. and Kibirige, J.S. (1989), 'Political violence and Eritrean health care', *Social Science and Medicine*, Vol. 28, No. 7, pp. 677-84.

Sivard, R.L. (1991), *World Military and Social Expenditures 1991*, World Priorities, Washington.

Smallman-Raynor, M. and Cliff, A. (1991), 'Civil war and the spread of AIDS in central Africa', *Epidemiology of Infectious Diseases*, Vol. 107, No. 1, pp. 69-80.

Stewart, F. (1993), 'War and underdevelopment: can economic analysis help reduce the costs?', *Journal of International Development*, Vol. 5, No. 4, pp. 357-80.

Stover, E., Keller, A.S., Cobey, J. and Sopheap, S. (1994), 'The medical and social consequences of land mines in Cambodia', *Journal of the American Medical Association*, Vol. 272, No. 5, pp. 331-6.

Summerfield, D. (1991), 'The psychosocial effects of conflict in the Third World', *Development in Practice*, Vol. 1, pp. 159-73.

Toole, M.J. (1994), 'The rapid assessment of health problems in refugee and displaced populations', *Medicine and Global Survival*, Vol. 1, pp. 200-7.

Toole, M.J. and Waldman, R.J. (1990), 'Prevention of excess mortality in refugee and displaced populations in developing countries', *Journal of the American Medical Association*, Vol. 263, No. 24, pp. 3296-302.

Toole, M.J. and Waldman, R.J. (1993), 'Refugee and displaced persons. War, hunger and public health', *Journal of the American Medical Association*, Vol. 270, No. 5, pp. 600-5.

UNICEF (1989), *Children on the Front Line. The impact of Apartheid, Destabilization and Warfare on Children in Southern and South Africa*, UNICEF, New York.

United Nations Development Programme (1994), *Human Development Report, 1994*, Oxford University Press, Oxford.

United Nations High Commissioner for Refugees (1993), *The State of the World's Refugees. The challenge of Protection*, Penguin Books, Harmondsworth.

Wallensteen, P. and Sollenberg, M. (1995), 'After the Cold War: Emerging patterns of armed conflict 1989-94', *Journal of Peace Research*, Vol. 32, No. 3, pp. 345-60.

Walt, G. and Cliff, J. (1986), 'The dynamics of health policies in Mozambique 1975-85', *Health Policy and Planning*, Vol. 1, No. 2, pp. 148-57.

Zwi, A. (1995), 'Commentary: Life in the real world is more complicated', *British Medical Journal*, Vol. 311, pp. 1001-2

Zwi, A. and Cabral, A.J.R. (1991), 'High risk situations for AIDS prevention', *British Medical Journal*, Vol. 303, pp. 1527-9.

Zwi, A. and Ugalde, A. (1989), 'Towards an epidemiology of political violence in the Third World', *Social Science and Medicine*, Vol. 28, No. 7, pp. 633-42.

Zwi, A. and Ugalde, A. (1991), 'Political violence and health in the Third World - a public health issue', *Health Policy and Planning*, Vol. 6, pp. 203-17.

7 Making violence useful

Simon Carter

Introduction

A number of years ago, while I was a student with the Open University, I attended a summer school for the social sciences. Our programme of study was complemented by guest lectures in the evenings. One of these was entitled 'the Sociology of Violence'. This particular lecture was one of the best attended of the week. However, despite this initial indication of popularity some were left feeling disappointed at the end. The lecturer had spent most of the talk explaining why the subject was difficult to research because defining violence often tends to slip into a listing by example rather than an exploration of meaning. As I was leaving the lecture a student, who was an officer in the Royal Ulster Constabulary, said 'I'd like to take him to Northern Ireland and see if he still had a problem defining violence'. While this comment was somewhat unfair (as it reinforced the point that the speaker was making) it does reflect a common and shared assumption. Namely that violence, as experienced personally, is easy to define. Furthermore, the tone of his and others' remarks indicated a feeling that academic researchers were wasting their time in attempting to define violence - they should be getting on with the real job of reducing something that is obviously evil.

Is the subject of violence this simple? While, at one level, there may be a general consensus that violence is something harmful there is also, at another level, the idea that violence may be justified or even useful in certain circumstances. Little agreement may exist about the conditions that need to be met in order for violence to be legitimate - this could be self-defence of the individual or to prevent a greater collective violence - but many people would endorse the view that in some predicaments violence is excusable or even necessary.

This chapter will be an exploration of this idea of useful violence, its place in our modern culture, and its decision making processes. This contribution to the debate on violence is not going to be particularly original, indeed it will repeat a story that has been told before, but I believe it is an important story that has too rarely been heard. First though, what do I mean by violence? Violence will here be defined as any damaging physical force. One of the problems with the way the word violence is used is that it can apply to both intentional and unintentional acts. An air disaster could be described as violent whether it resulted from mistake (e.g. mechanical failure) or intention (e.g. a bomb). There is also a third possibility, that it was the result of a mistake that was known about in advance. On March 3, 1974, a DC-10 aircraft, manufactured by McDonnell Douglas, crashed on the outskirts of Paris with a loss of 346 lives. The cause was found to be a faulty cargo door that had opened during the flight, causing an explosive decompression of the aircraft cabin. This seemed to be a case of violence following from a mistake. Yet in the years from 1969 to 1974 McDonnell Douglas had received five independent warnings that there may have been a problem with the design of this door (Perrow, 1984, p.139). So while this violence was not intentional, it was a conscious outcome of a decision process; in this case the decision not to rectify a known problem that had the potential to lead to multiple fatalities. It is this conscious use of violence, either through intent or inaction, that I intend to consider here.

I do not intend to discuss individual acts of violence but rather those forms of violence that could be seen as collective. By this I mean any action or decision taken by a group, institution or organization that leads to a damaging use of force. I have chosen to concentrate on collective forms of violence because over the last three decades there has been a large amount of research into violence which has looked at individual acts. Some of this work only takes the individual as its starting point but then proceeds to consider the structural relations behind individual acts of violence. For instance, feminist research has considered male violence from the point of view of the lived experience of women who have been exposed to it. In the process, common definitions of violence have been problematized in order to argue that individual male acts of violence act to the benefit of patriarchy as a whole. Other approaches, that start with the individual, have been less capable of moving from the individual act of violence to a level of understanding that takes cultural context into consideration. A good example here is the debate within psychology about the presumed causal relationship between consumption of particular cultural products (such as videos) and actual acts of violence.

Rationality and violence

Within the social sciences there has been little attention paid to the topic of collective violence and the ways in which such violence is made useful. Often under these circumstances violence is not even defined as such. Consideration of these forms of violence is uncomfortable because to do so is also to acknowledge the suggestion that the modern desire for safety, security and order ultimately leads to brutality. Moreover, this is not some temporary aberration, error or pathology but, rather, it is a routine outcome of those formalized knowledges that seek to manage danger and uncertainty.

One social scientist who has addressed some of these issues, in an analysis of the Holocaust, is the sociologist Zygmunt Bauman (1989). His account begins by asking how it is that the subject of the Holocaust has received so little attention from the social sciences. For the most part social research and theory continues as if the Holocaust was a fleeting incident in the continuation of history. How is it that a violence of this magnitude is either left to historians and theologians, or is marginalized into its own specialist subject area? The answer Bauman provides is that a closer study of the Holocaust would undermine key foundations of the social sciences in a way that the study of few other subjects could. This is because the social sciences still largely retain the etiological myth - the belief in an emergence from a pre-social barbarity into a civilized and rational society. Within this view the Holocaust is conceived as a defeat of civilization to restrain the last remaining vestiges of a pre-social cruelty - it was a temporary fall from action as guided by modern rationality. The perpetrators of the Holocaust were irrational monsters feeding off a long history of Germanic anti-Semitism.

Unfortunately historical research does not support this comforting myth. Rather, Bauman finds an alternative interpretation to be more credible. The Holocaust was an event that 'contains crucial information about the society of which we are *all* members' (Bauman, 1989, p. xiv). At the centre of the analysis we must place some of the most highly regarded facets of our own culture and civilization; 'its technology, its rational criteria of choice, its tendency to subordinate thought and action to the pragmatics of economy and effectiveness' (Bauman, 1989, p. 13). The Holocaust did not enter modern history after the re-surfacing of irrational emotions. It appeared in the guise of a modern industrial system, using knowledge that only science could provide, and pursuing a program created by scientifically managed organizations. The Holocaust was not a predestined outcome of modern civilization but it was 'the rational world of modern civilization that made the Holocaust thinkable' (Bauman, 1989, p. 13). Without the technological and scientific methods of our industrial society it would not have been possible. In particular, the modern tendency to regard society as an object amenable to principles of engineering and management (such as social engineering and control) led to the use of violence as the most efficient and cost-effective means to meet instrumental-rational criteria. Under such circumstances the moral evaluation of ends are easily detached from means:

> The most shattering of lessons deriving from the analysis of the 'twisted road to Auschwitz' is that - in the last resort - the choice of physical extermination as the right means to the task of *Entfernung* was a product of a routine bureaucratic procedures: means-ends, calculus, budget balancing, universal rule application ... At no point of its long and tortuous execution did the Holocaust come in conflict with the principles of rationality. The 'Final Solution' did not clash at any stage with the rational pursuit of efficient, optimal goal implementation. On the contrary, it arose out of a genuinely rational concern (Bauman, 1989, p. 17).

The Holocaust was never inevitable, it was one potential that our modern society made possible. Our culture's institutions and decision making processes were powerless to stop it. Yet it is not just that they were ineffective in halting the violence. It is more than this. The long chain of decisions that led to the attempted genocide of European Jewry were guided at every stage by ways of thinking and management of society that were, and still are, entirely normal and commonplace - namely scientific reason and rational judgement.

One of the principles that has guided scientific action and reasoning since the Enlightenment is that the scientific endeavour is about discovery of the truth, of the facts and of objectivity. Such a pursuit has meant that there was both a separation from the normative obligations demanded by ethics or religion and also a separation from any conflict brought about by emotion. It has often been pointed out by historians that science has been fabricated around a series of similar dichotomies: objectivity versus subjectivity; culture versus nature; rationality versus irrationality; mind versus body. Moreover, this division of understanding is not weighted impartially; the former terms are fabricated as useful, as the operators of science, whereas the latter terms are what science operates on. But such a split means that the very terms that may allow us to make decisions about moral issues become blurred into instrumental and rational criteria. Violence becomes one more useful tool that under certain circumstances (dictated by rationality) becomes the most efficient means of solving a problem. The event of the Holocaust should have alerted us to this fact but, as Bauman rightly points out, it is a warning that has largely gone unheeded.

The Holocaust was a unique and terrible event but our desire to hold on to the 'fall from civilization' myth rather than seeing it as part of modern civilization, covers up important lessons that may be learned. The period since the Second World War has seen instrumental and rational criteria used to produce outcomes that are not on the same scale as the Holocaust but which still see violence as a useful tool for solving social dilemmas. Two particular types of modern rational knowledge and decision making lend themselves to outcomes that view violence as an allowable effect in the search for solutions to problems: the trading of costs and the search for neutral problem solving knowledge. First I will consider the cost approach. Even as the Second World War was drawing to a close the allies (led by the Americans) applied the rational balancing of costs as a justification for the use of atomic weapons. The bombing of Hiroshima and Nagasaki came at the end of an extremely violent conflict in the Pacific. According to one argument, if the war had been allowed to continue many more may have died on both the American and Japanese sides. It was therefore reasonable to use some violence in order to prevent a greater loss of life.

The reasoning behind this decision making process involves a balancing trick. If the consequences of two alternative courses of action can be compared then the outcome with the lowest cost is the preferable course of action. In the example above the costs were measured in human lives; a more common measure of cost is in simple economic terms. Either way, a form of logic which says 'if we do this then *n* people will die, whereas if we do the other then *n x 2* will die' becomes very difficult to resist, except on the grounds of faulty methods used to calculate the numbers. This is because the scope of such decision making does not ever move away from the numbers game of rational choice. To reach a rational choice concerning two different courses of action we need to be able to compare them directly in a quantifiable and neutral way. Some artefacts are very easy to measure and compare numerically (such as deaths or money). However, other qualities are virtually impossible either to quantify or compare. How does one go about comparing the morality of suddenly incinerating a large number of civilians against the morality of a long drawn out conflict with very large numbers of dead?

Costs benefits and violence

The period after the Second World War saw a swift expansion of the cost approach to decision making. In the post war era the principal reason for this was the growth of a variety of novel issues and risks, often of a technological nature. Decision makers became faced with the problem of managing complex problems without historical precedent as a guide. The past was no longer an adequate guide for the future - there was simply not enough of it. Since the end of the Second World War a new profession of the expert risk assessor has matured largely in the shape of 'risk benefit' or 'cost benefit analysis' (CBA). One of the first problems was connected with the Second World War itself. This was the question of how to manage the new generation of nuclear weapons. This was where CBA first enjoyed widespread use, within American nuclear 'defence'. The problem was one of allocating resources to the purchase of a 'credible' nuclear strike force and of calculating under what circumstances such weapons of mass destruction should be used. CBA was used extensively, together with game theory, by the Pentagon to provide answers to these questions.

The experts charged with operating these new tools have produced an interdisciplinary quasi-profession with it's own terminology, methodology, and literature. They perform many functions, including: to advise and inform about the best strategy for coping with future risks; to determine what risks are acceptable by attempting to weigh future losses against future gains; and more frequently, at least from a cynical point of view, to 'legitimate the decisions of elites in the private and public sectors' (Perrow, 1984, p. 307). This type of analysis often uses sophisticated and esoteric mathematical models such as: Bayesian probabilities; probability density functions; discounted future probabilities; Monte Carlo techniques; stratum-specific attributable risks; and beta-binomial distributions. Such methods have the effect of separating the decision process from a method that is more public and open to inspection.

Of course the decisions relating to issues such as the use of nuclear weapons could have been left to more democratic processes. But at some stage this would have involved inviting people to consider issues relating to their use. Asking people what their risk preferences were, under these circumstances, was avoided for two reasons: first, the lay public is depicted by the practitioners and experts of CBA as irrational and biased in judgements about risk. Thus, the lay public are seen as unfit to make such decisions (see Perrow, 1984); Secondly, for policy makers to prompt the opinion of the populace may have brought about a more public debate concerning the cost, dangers and use of nuclear weapons - a debate that policy makers would probably wish to avoid.

One of the main questions that CBA has sought to answer is what constitutes an acceptable risk. From an economic point of view, the idea of total safety is unattainable. This is because it is argued that safety is a normal good which is purchased, in the market-place, like any other good. Thus, following the classic rules of economics, we can only have more safety, and less danger, at the expense of giving up other things. In order to produce an extra unit of safety the costs do not increase in a uniform manner. After some point the cost of producing more safety increases more and more rapidly. The point where the costs of prevention (that is, the benefits) balance the cost to society is known as the 'optimum level of risk' (the dotted line in Figure 7.1).

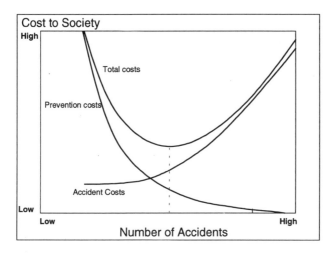

Figure 7.1 The costs of risk (accident and prevention costs) versus number of accidents
Source: Starr, 1976

The above explanation of cost benefit analysis (and the associated graph) may give the impression that the technique operates in some egalitarian way - it talks of costs to society as a whole, as if there was some general consultation process. This rarely occurs because, as we have seen, such decisions require the use of rational methods unavailable to the general public. Thus judgement is left to the experts who work for powerful institutions and organizations. For example, in the early 1970s the Ford Motor Company was developing a new 'compact' car, the Pinto. The designers had two choices concerning the placement of the fuel tank. One involved placing the tank at the rear of the car and the other would place the tank towards the middle of the car. With the rear positioning there was a greater possibility that in accidents the tank would rupture and consequently the occupants would burn. However, positioning the tank in the middle of the car would cost more to manufacture. The decision was made to position the tank at the rear of the car. After an accident, in which a Pinto did ignite and burn its occupants, and the ensuing lawsuit, some of Ford's internal memos came to light. These showed that a cost benefit analysis had been performed which balanced the costs of modifying the Pinto against the compensation that would have to be paid to victims. Costs of changing the car were almost three times greater than the 'benefits' and so production went ahead with the fuel tank in the more dangerous position[1].

This example is not chosen to single out the Ford Motor Company for particular criticism, but rather to illustrate how any manufacturer would behave. Manufacturers have to price their products to cover costs and one of the costs will generally be lawsuits against them. Within the rational model of decision making the most valid criticism that could be made of Ford was that they got their sums wrong - they made a mistake with their valuation of a statistical life. But what is apparent is that the consumers who bought cars of this type were never given the choice to set their own risk preferences. What is more, any valuation of this type, which attempts to evaluate the probability of death in economic terms, will see violence as one useful choice open to decision makers. It will be economically useful to allow some people to die in violent circumstances.

In the above example the decision making was performed by a private company to their own advantage. It would not be expected that a commercial organization, operating in an economy based on profit, would act in the general interests of society. However, in the last two decades cost benefit analysis has been used by governments in exactly this way - as a tool to judge the overall good of particular projects. As Adams has pointed out, the underlying axiom on which CBA is used in these circumstances is the search for a 'Pareto improvement' (Adams, 1995). This is the probability that some people (at least one) will benefit but no one lose. This may be an exceptional situation, so a 'potential' Pareto is normally looked for instead - one where the winners 'compensate the losers out of their winnings and still leave something over' (Adams, 1995, p. 95). But how are the winners and losers to be judged? The normal means is to resort to economic criteria.

The use of economic criteria presents a problem for the decision maker. Suppose a government wishes to build a motorway (or a nuclear reprocessing plant, the actual example is immaterial). Those people living near the proposed development may regard themselves as losers. For the potential Pareto improvement to be realised they must be compensated for their loss. The obvious way to judge the amount of this compensation is to ask them how much they are *willing to accept* as a settlement. If, however, someone claims that no amount will compensate them for their loss then they are effectively setting their willingness to accept as close to infinity. Under these circumstances a potential Pareto improvement is not possible. Cost benefit analysis therefore asks a slightly different question: how much would they be *prepared to pay* to prevent the loss. The amount one can pay is wholly different from an amount one is willing to accept - one is finite and the other can be infinite. Thus the sum that a person is 'willing and able to pay to prevent loss will rarely be an accurate measure of that loss the person is experiencing' (Adams, 1995, p. 99). This is particularly true where the loss in question is human life. Given the choice of putting a monetary value on compensation for loss of one's life the rational response would be to claim an infinite amount. However, if the valuation is of the cost one is able to pay, or that someone is able to pay on your behalf, to prevent a specific probability of early death then the problem becomes soluble. Yet the losers in this calculation will be unlikely to feel compensated. Decision making of this type cannot but fail to be implicated in doing violence to those who are less able to pay, or unable to find someone to pay on their behalf, to prevent their own deaths.

The full scope of this logic can be considered if we see how it is applied to a real problem. Recently there has been widespread concern about the effects of global warming. While it is still too early to make predictions about whether, and at what rate, global warming is happening, there is a definite possibility that the global temperature is rising. This could result in the partial melting of polar ice caps and the flooding of low lying areas. If global warming is taking place then the most probable cause is CO_2 emissions, which by and large come from Western industrial nations and are directly connected to economic growth. One question that governments, and policy makers, have considered is whether Western nations should slow down their emissions of CO_2.

As is often the case with cost benefit calculations, the winners and losers are not from the same group. Western nations stand to benefit from continued CO_2 emissions because they gain the most from economic growth. On the other hand, losers will be those nonindustrialized nations who have had little advantage from growth and will be worst placed to deal with rising sea levels. To use CBA to make a decision about this we would have to find out the amount of money that people in nonindustrialized nations would accept to lose their homes and livelihoods. The problems identified above make CBA unusable if only one person answers that no amount can provide compensation for such a loss. Delegates at the 1993 International Conference on the Economics of Climate Change (Adams, 1995, p. 173) found a way round this problem. The costs used in the analysis were not remuneration for damage that might happen in places like Bangladesh, but the cost of not continuing with economic growth in the West. Thus, failure to pursue continued economic growth is set against current land values in nonindustrialized nations. When a risk calculation is set up in this way the

133

rational response is to legitimize violence against players who were never given the chance to enter the game on an equal footing. As Adams sums the situation up:

> In this analysis, the rich nations on board the juggernaut do not ask those whom they are about to obliterate, 'what sum of money would leave you feeling as well off after we have run over you as before?' They ask, in effect, 'what would your country fetch if offered for sale in the open market without planning permission for development?' (Adams, 1995, p. 174).

The search for knowledge and violence

We have seen how the cost approach to decision making uses instrumental rational criteria to legitimate projects in which winners and losers remain unequal. Moreover, this tends tacitly to authorize effects which the recipients will experience as violent. The language of CBA tends to obscure this fact by only considering elements that can be reduced to a numerical value.

If we now consider the second way in which instrumental and rational criteria can lead to violence - the search for objective problem solving knowledge - we can see a similar process of balancing gains against contingent losses. The post war period has seen the invention of a number of new technologies where historical experience provides few clues about the best way to manage them. These would include nuclear technology (both civil and military applications), electronic transfer of information, genetic engineering, and certain industrial production techniques (for instance, pesticide production). Here the problem of assessment is made problematic by dint of the fact that the costs and benefits are often unknown. The problem is with the transfer of an innovation, produced under laboratory settings, to the general environment. Under such circumstances the general environment often becomes an extension of the laboratory - the place where final testing of costs and benefits are carried out.

One of the most prolific and violent examples of the environment being used as a test site for technical innovation is the post war experiments with nuclear weapons. In the period from 1951 to 1963 American government[2] scientists and military personnel detonated 126 atomic bombs in the atmosphere over their Nevada test site. Each of these explosions discharged similar amounts of radiation into the environment as was released from the Chernobyl nuclear reactor accident in 1986. After the Chernobyl disaster it was estimated that more than 100,000 people were exposed to high levels of radioactivity (Saenger, 1986). The cost of this venture was the damage done, on both a local and global scale, to human populations and habitats. The benefit of the program was the gaining of medical and scientific knowledge of how the West may prevail in a nuclear war. The benefits were thought to be well worth the price paid in human suffering. Until recently the Nevada tests did not receive the same high profile media coverage as Chernobyl. This was because such nuclear tests were surrounded by high levels of secrecy. But this secrecy also helped secure a freedom to carry out experiments, no matter how damaging they were to the environment and those who inhabited it:

> In their highly centralised industrial bureaucracy, protected by strict military secrecy, atomic scientists were free to take any risk, conduct any test, and set up any experiment without outside interference. No matter the violence that would occur to land or the people, the leaders of the Atomic Energy Commission ... believed that their actions if uncovered would be justified by history (Schneider, 1993, p. xvi).

It is difficult to comprehend fully the scale of the violence enacted on those people who worked and lived in areas of these nuclear experiments. Much has been written about the effects that nuclear testing had on those who were exposed to them. One of the most powerful accounts is that recorded by Carole Gallagher in her book *American Ground Zero: The Secret Nuclear War* (Gallagher, 1993). This book is a photo record and oral history of people who worked on and who lived downwind of the test sites (know as the 'downwinders'). Gallagher forces one to picture the unimaginable - a government which launches an undeclared war on its own people. Her account does not allow the reader any retreat into a rational balancing of costs and benefits as a justification for violence. But the account does show that such ideas were prevalent amongst government institutions and organizations. Residents, and those working on the test projects, were continually told that there was no danger and even encouraged to watch fallout clouds by coming outside of their homes, to 'participate in a moment of history'. One of the military personnel involved in the test programme, a Colonel Langford Harrison, summed up the alliance of cost justification with secrecy prevalent at this time:

> That's what war is, a calculated risk. You know somebody is going to get killed ... Some may die of cancer, some may be all right, we don't know. No one's ever done it before but we'll take the risk for the evolvement and improvement of the weapon system. The information was either withheld purposely or accidentally, but I have to say purposely... The whole thing was fraught with peril and danger and they knew it was, and this I resent quite readily (quoted in Gallagher, 1993, p. 97).

In Atomic Energy Commission documents the downwinders, living in Utah and Nevada, were defined as 'a low use segment of the population'. Bomb tests were always timed so that the wind was in the 'right' direction - towards the populations of Utah and away from those of Las Vegas and Los Angles. One official when questioned by Gallagher about this practice, of waiting until the wind blew to Utah before testing bombs, said, on tape, 'those people in Utah don't give a shit about radiation'. The combination of secrecy and repeated assurances that all was well led many of those featured in Gallagher's account to believe they had been used as secret guinea pigs. Martha Bordoli Laird, living in a sparsely populated part of Nevada, was typical. She knew many locals who had died of cancer (including her own two children):

> I could name a hundred people living along that line where someone, somewhere has died of cancer. I mean around this area ... I will always believe that fallout had a lot to do with it. No way, in my mind, will ever erase that. We are the forgotten guinea pigs (quoted in Gallagher, 1993, p. 97).

When in 1957 she wrote to her senator asking for information about her son's death she received the following reply:

> A large segment of the scientific world is in disagreement with the government's nuclear testing program ... This has resulted in a fallout scare ... The President has questioned these reports coming from a minority group of scientists ... it is not impossible to suppose that some of these 'scare' stories are communist inspired. If they could get us to agree not to use the only weapon with which we could win a war, the conquest of Europe and Asia would be easy (quoted in Gallagher, 1993, p. 118).

As Gallagher says in her introduction, 'each society produces its own slaughter of innocents, of those who are most expendable in dangerous times, whether danger is falsely manufactured to achieve a political end or truly exists' (Gallagher, 1993, p. xxxi). The people who lived in the vicinity of the nuclear test sites (and the many service men who were intentionally exposed to nuclear blasts) were thought to be expendable in the program to develop weapons for the nuclear age. Every one of the personal accounts from Gallagher's book tells of a people who were subjected to intentional violence and misinformation. Such as Elmer Pickett, a local mortician who lost sixteen members of his family to cancer and had to develop special embalming techniques to cope with the small gaunt and bloodless bodies of cancer victims. Or Eugene Hayes, a test site security guard who was ordered to within a quarter of a mile of ground zero immediately after a nuclear explosion to 'guard' plutonium balls. After this incident the media became interested in his case. Before a press conference he was put under pressure to withhold facts about his case. If he agreed to say that it was his fault, and that he had taken a wrong turn, then he would be offered a job for life. His wife (and later widow) Sarah recalled what happened at the press conference and after:

> A woman from Sweden asked him, 'How can you be so stupid as to go down the wrong road?' He just broke down and cried, he couldn't even answer her. They closed off the mikes then ... Gene worked about a month and they let him go. Gene asked 'What about the promise of a lifetime job?'. Captain McIntyre said 'Prove it'. I'm talking about callous men, not men with compassion. Things quieted down, Gene was no longer news, the tests were going on, other people were irradiated. We were never right. They were always right (Gallagher, 1993, p. 39).

Conclusion

This essay has shown that many of the common methods, used by institutions and organizations to take decisions about how to manage the future lead to the conscious use of violence. This violence is often justified because an alternative course of action may lead to a greater loss. But this balancing of costs and benefits seeks to compare objects that are essentially distinct and therefore not comparable. One way in which such objects can apparently be rendered comparable is to reduce them to numerical measures, usually of economic worth. The reducing of complex social phenomena to numerical costs cannot but fail to push important human values out of the decision process. Ideas such as justice, equality and ethics are not easy to incorporate into the rational decision making process.

What is more, such decision making processes are taken by small groups of experts working for powerful institutions. This has meant that in the post war period judgement has become increasingly displaced from the range of those who are subjected to violence. Judgement is depoliticized because it is not open to negotiation. Instead judgement becomes 'a calculated risk' in the untied hands of experts confident 'that their actions if uncovered would be justified by history'.

This is a bleak and pessimistic view of the modern society and its decision making processes. If we accept that we live in an increasingly interdependent world with complex social structures then we must also accept that we need ways of making collective decisions about the future and the dangers it may hold. By now we should also know that putting total faith in rationality as the only tool to make such decisions leads to violence. The subjects of morality and ethics need to be put back into decision making. This will not be an easy process as moral issues do not fare well when faced with the power of rational interest. Bauman's concluding remarks to his account of the Holocaust point towards two lessons that can be learnt from history. I finish by quoting them at length:

> *In a system where rationality and ethics point in opposite directions, humanity is the main loser.* Evil can do its dirty work, hoping that most people most of the time will refrain from doing rash, reckless things - and resisting evil is rash and reckless. Evil needs neither enthusiastic followers nor an applauding audience - the instinct of self-preservation will do, encouraged by the comforting thought that it is not my turn yet, thank God: by lying low, I can escape...
>
> The second lesson tells us that putting self-preservation above moral duty is in no way predetermined, inevitable and inescapable. One can be pressed to do it, but one cannot be forced to do it, and thus one cannot really shift the responsibility for doing it on those who exerted the pressure. It does not matter how many people chose moral duty over the rationality of self-preservation - what counts is that some did. Evil is not all-powerful. It can be resisted. The testimony of the few who did resist shatters the authority of the logic of self-preservation. It shows it for what it is in the end - a choice. One wonders how many people must defy that logic for evil to be incapacitated. Is there a magic threshold of defiance beyond which technology of evil grinds to a halt? (Bauman, 1989, p. 224)

Notes

1. In the original calculations the costs of lawsuits were estimated to be $49.5 million (180 burn deaths, 180 serious burn injuries, 2100 burnt vehicles) and the costs of modification were estimated to be $137 million ($11 per car). In 1977 the Santa Anna Superior Court awarded $128 million to Richard Grimshaw after he received 90 per cent burns in a Pinto (Dowie and Pym 1980, p.40-41).
2. Similar tests were carried out by the Soviet, French and UK governments in this period. The American case is considered here because these secret tests have been made public in Federal Courts.

Bibliography

Adams, J. (1995), *Risk*, UCL Press, London.

Bauman, Z. (1989), *Modernity and the Holocaust*, Polity, Oxford.

Bauman, Z. (1993), *Postmodern Ethics*, Blackwell, Oxford.

Dowie, J. and Pym, C. (1980), 'Risk to life and limb' in The Open University (eds.), *Risk: A Second Level Course*, The Open University, Milton Keynes, pp. 5-54.

Gallagher, C. (1993), *American Ground Zero: The Secret Nuclear War*, The MIT Press, Cambridge.

Massumi, B. (1992), 'Everywhere you want to be: introduction to Fear', *Warwick Journal of Philosophy*, Vol. 4, pp. 175-217.

Perrow, C. (1984), *Normal Accidents: Living with High Risk Technologies*, Basic Books, New York.

Saenger, E.L. (1986), 'Radiation accidents', *Annals of Emergency Medicine*, Vol. 15, pp. 1061-6.

Schneider, K. (1993), 'Foreword' to Gallagher, C. (1993), *American Ground Zero: The Secret Nuclear War*, The MIT Press, Cambridge.

Starr, C. (1976), 'General philosophy and risk-benefit analysis' in Ashley, H., Rdman, R. and Whipple, C. (ed.s), *Energy and the Environment: A Risk Benefit Approach*, Pergamon, Oxford, pp. 2-30.

Index

141